Let's Geopolitics Now

A Simple Guide to Exploring the Globe

from 2000 to 2021

by

Antonella Silipigni

An Introductory Guide to Geopolitics, with a brief analysis and summary of the significant milestones of the past twenty years in international politics and global political strategy, to help beginners take their first steps in this field.

Second Edition

ISBN: 9798377227366

Imprint: Independently published

"So, let's not just focus on our differences but also think about our common interests and how to overcome those differences. And if our differences cannot be resolved today, at least we can try to make the world a safe place for diversity. Because, at the end of the day, our most basic connection is that we all inhabit this little planet, breathe the same air, worry about our children's future, and we're all mortal."

J.F. Kennedy

INDEX

INTRODUCTION

Geopolitics is a vast and complex field that deals with the interactions and relationships between states, nations, and regions worldwide.

In the last twenty years, the world has seen a series of events and developments that have significantly impacted geopolitics and global political strategy.

In this introductory guide, we will examine some of the critical milestones of this period and attempt to provide an overview of the last twenty years' major geopolitical trends and challenges.

I aim to provide a basic understanding of geopolitics. I also hope to spark interest and curiosity in our readers to love this fascinating and essential field and encourage young people to pursue this profession.

PART ONE

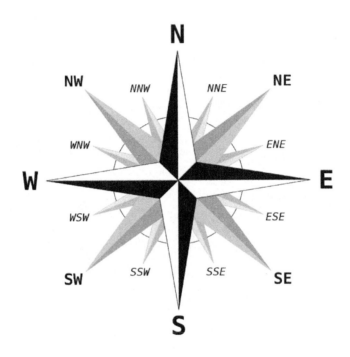

WHY IS IT IMPORTANT TO UNDERSTAND GEOPOLITICS?

Geopolitics is a discipline that studies the influence of geographical characteristics and location on politics and international strategy.

This includes the analysis of the relationships between geographical space and political and strategic activities, such as international relations, national security, global economy and environmental protection.

Geopolitics is crucial because it helps us understand how a place's geography, such as location, natural resources, climate, and landscape, influences politics and international strategy.

Geopolitics helps us understand:

- How a country's natural resources can affect its economy and place in the world
- How a country's geographical location can influence its national security and relationship with other countries.

Geopolitics helps us understand how a country's political and strategic choices can, in turn, influence its geography and place in the world. For example, policy choices on energy or economic development can significantly impact a country's geography, such as extracting natural resources or building infrastructure.

THE ORIGIN OF GEOPOLITICS

The history of geopolitics as a modern discipline begins in the late 19th century. However, some underlying ideas can be traced back to past thinkers such as Sun Tzu and Tacitus. One of the founders of modern geopolitics is the German geographer Friedrich Ratzel. He developed the theory of "Lebensraum" (living space), according to which a state needed to expand to meet the needs of its population and natural resources.

In the 18th century, German geographer Alexander von Humboldt and English political scientist Halford Mackinder began to study how geography influences politics and relationships between states. However, geopolitics as a modern discipline was primarily developed in the 19th and 20th centuries, particularly in Europe.

One of the first theorists of modern geopolitics was German geographer Friedrich Ratzel. He argued that the state needed to expand to survive, and that geography played an important role in determining a state's expansion opportunities. Another influential geopolitical theorist was British political scientist Halford Mackinder, who argued that controlling the central regions of Eurasia was crucial for global domination.

HOW IS GEOPOLITICS USED TO STUDY THE RELATIONSHIPS BETWEEN GEOGRAPHICAL SPACE AND POLITICS?

Geopolitics is a discipline that studies the influence of geographical features and location on politics and international strategy. This includes the analysis of the relationships between geographical space and political and strategic activities, such as international relations, national security, global economy, and environmental protection.

Geopolitics is used to study the relationships between geographical space and politics by analysing how the geographical characteristics of a place, such as location, natural resources, climate and landscape, affect politics and international strategy.

Geopolitics is also used to study how a country's political and strategic choices can, in turn, affect its geography and its role in the world. For example, policy choices in energy or economic development can significantly impact a country's geography, such as extracting natural resources or constructing infrastructure.

Geopolitics is used to study the relationships between geographical space and politics in various ways.

Generally, Geopolitics analyses how analyses affect political relationships and government decisions. This can include how to analyse location, natural resources, borders, and other geographical factors that affect the politics of a region or country.

Geopolitics can also be used to study how relations between states can be influenced by geography and natural resources and how such connections can, in turn, affect global peace and stability.

It can be used to predict future developments in international political relations and to understand the motivations behind government policy decisions.

Geopolitics experts often use various data sources such as maps, demographic statistics, economic data and intelligence reports to study these relationships. They can also conduct qualitative research, such as interviews with experts or analysis of official documents.

Geopolitics experts can use these data sources to develop theories and models to understand the relationships between geographical space and politics.

In summary, Geopolitics is used to study the relationships between geographical area and politics by analysing the influence of geographical characteristics on politics and international strategy and the impact of political and strategic choices on a place's geography.

EXPLORING HOW GEOPOLITICS IS USED IN THE CURRENT INTERNATIONAL POLITICAL AND STRATEGIC CONTEXT.

Here are some ways in which Geopolitics is used in the current international political and strategic context:

● Analysis of the impact of a country's natural resources on its economy and its position in the world.

● Study a country's geographical position and influence on its national security and relationship with other countries.

● Analysis of the impact of a country's political and strategic choices on its geography and its position in the world.

● Understanding the impact of human activities on geography and international politics, such as climate change or exploitation of natural resources.

● Analysis of the impact of information and communication technology on international politics and strategy.

● Study of the influence of geographical features on the formation of alliances.

HOW CONTEMPORARY GEOPOLITICS IS USED IN VARIOUS WAYS IN THE CURRENT INTERNATIONAL POLITICAL AND STRATEGIC CONTEXT

For National Security

For example, Geopolitics experts often analyze how a region's geography and natural resources can affect national security and political stability. They may also study how relationships between states can be influenced by geography and how those relationships can, in turn, affect global peace and tranquillity.

Contemporary Geopolitics is used to understand the motivations behind the government's political decisions and to predict future global political relations developments. For example, Geopolitics experts can analyze how access to natural resources, such as oil or gas, may influence a region's or country's politics.

For Military Defense

Contemporary Geopolitics is also used in military strategy and national defence. For example, Geopolitics experts can analyze how the geography of a region can affect a state's strategic position or its ability to defend against external threats. In addition, geopolitics is often used in planning overseas military missions to understand how the geography of a region can affect a state's ability to conduct effective military operations.

For International Trade Relations

Geopolitics is used in the analysis of international trade relations. For example, Geopolitics experts can analyze how the geography of a region can affect its attractiveness for foreign investment or its ability to export products.

Geopolitics can also be used to understand how a region's geography and natural resources can influence trade relations.

HOW GEOPOLITICS ANALYZES: HOW DO GEOGRAPHICAL POSITION, NATURAL RESOURCES, BORDERS AND OTHER GEOGRAPHICAL FACTORS INFLUENCE POLITICAL RELATIONS AND GOVERNMENT DECISIONS?

Here are some points on how Geopolitics analyzes how geographical position, natural resources, borders and other geographical factors influence political relations and government decisions:

• **Geographical position:** A state's geographical position can influence the national security and political stability. For example, a state in a strategic position may have more significant opportunities for trade relations with other states or be able to defend against external threats.

• **Natural resources:** A state's natural resources can influence political relations and government decisions. For example, a state with resources such as oil or gas may have greater bargaining power with other states or may be able to exploit these resources to increase its eco.

- **Borders:** A state's borders can influence political relations and government decisions. For example, a state with shared borders with other states may have more significant trade relations opportunities to project cross-border conflicts.

- **Natural resources** of a state can influence its attractiveness for foreign investment or its ability to generate income. For example, a state with large reserve oil or gas reserves.

In Geopolitics, several other geographical factors can influence political relations and government decisions. Here is a list of some of these factors:

- Climate

- Topography

- Access to the sea

- Natural resources (such as oil, gas, and water)

- Proximity to other nations

- Infrastructures and Transportation

- Natural Disasters

- Population density and distribution

- Natural resources (water, gas, oil etc.)

WHAT IS REQUIRED TO BE-COME AN EXPERT IN GEOPOLITICS?

To become an expert in Geopolitics: it is essential to have a solid understanding of some fundamental concepts, such as:

Geography: it is vital to know the geography, including the natural elements such as continents, oceans, mountain ranges and rivers, and artificial features such as cities, infrastructures and borders.

History: it is essential to know the history of relationships between states and how geography has influenced them over time.

Politics: it is essential to have a solid understanding of political institutions and the dynamics of international politics.

Economics: it is essential to understand how the economy affects Geopolitics and how Geopolitics can affect the economy.

International relations: it is essential to understand relationships between states and how these relationships can be influenced by geography and natural resources.

Data analysis: collecting and analysing qualitative and quantitative data is essential to understand geopolitical dynamics.

Communication: it is essential to communicate one's analysis and conclusions clearly and concisely.

To become an expert in Geopolitics, undertaking a suitable course of study and training is necessary.

Here are some steps you can follow to become an expert in Geopolitics:

Start with basic training: To become an expert in Geopolitics: it is essential to have a solid basic knowledge of different disciplines, such as history, geography, economics and political science. You can obtain this knowledge by attending undergraduate courses in these disciplines or by reading books and articles on these topics.

Specialize your training: Once you have acquired a solid basic knowledge, you can specialize your training in Geopolitics. There are various options to specialize in this discipline, such as a bachelor's degree in Geopolitics or a Master's degree in Geopolitics.

Continue to study and gain experience: To become an expert in Geopolitics: it is essential to continue researching and gaining experience in the field. There are various ways to do this, such as:

- Attending updated courses or conferences on Geopolitics

- Reading books and articles on Geopolitics

• Doing internships or working in companies or organizations that deal with Geopolitics

• Conducting research or publishing articles on Geopolitics

• Develop your professional skills: To become an expert in Geopolitics, developing your professional skills is crucial. Various skills can be helpful in this field, such as:

○ Data analysis and interpretation skills

○ Writing and presentation skills

○ Knowledge of the English language and other foreign languages

○ Ability to work in teams and collaborate with other professionals

It is also essential to keep up to date with current events and developments in Geopolitics. This can be achieved by reading news articles, attending conferences, or joining professional organizations focusing on Geopolitics.

Some famous experts in Geopolitics

Here is a chronological list of some of the world's most respected geopolitical experts:

• Halford Mackinder (1861-1947): was an early geopolitical scholar and developed the "Heart of the World" theory, which argued that control of the central regions of Eurasia was crucial to world domination.

• Nicholas J. Spykman (1893-1943): was an American geopolitical scholar who developed the "Ring Belt" theory, which argued that control of the regions surrounding Eurasia was fundamental to world domination.

• Hans Morgenthau (1904-1980): was one of the most influential geopolitical scholars of the 20th century and developed the theory of "Political Realism," which argues that states primarily act based on their national interests.

• Zbigniew Brzezinski (1928-2017): American political strategist and geopolitical scholar. He was the National Security Advisor for President Jimmy Carter. He wrote numerous books on geopolitics, including "The Grand Chessboard" and "The Choice: Global Domination or Global Leadership".

• Robert D. Kaplan (born 1952): is an American writer and journalist known for his writings on geopolitics. He has written numerous books on geopolitics, including "The Revenge of Geography" and "The Coming Anarchy".

• John Mearsheimer (born 1947): an American political scientist known for his geopolitics and international relations studies. He has written numerous books on geopolitics, including "The Tragedy of Great Power Politics" and "The Israel Lobby and U.S. Foreign Policy".

• Kishore Mahbubani (born 1948): are a diplomat and geopolitical scholar from Singapore. He has written numerous books on geopolitics, including "The New Asian Hemisphere" and "The Great Convergence: Asia, the West, and the Logic of One World".

• Parag Khanna (born 1970): are an Indian American writer and geopolitical scholar. He has written numerous books on geopolitics, including "Connectography: Mapping the Future of Global Civilization" and "The Future is Asian: Commerce, Conflict, and Culture in the 21st Century".

WHAT ARE THE DIFFERENCES BETWEEN GEOPOLITICS, INTERNATIONAL POLITICS, AND INTERNATIONAL POLITICAL STRATEGY?

Geopolitics is the study of the influence of geography on politics and international relations. Geopolitics analyzes how geographical location, natural resources, borders, and other geographical factors affect government policy and decisions.

International politics is the study of international relations and their influence on politics. International politics analyzes how nations and international organizations interact and how their politics affect global politics.

International political strategy is the planning and implementation of specific actions to achieve political goals at the international level. Global political strategy can include diplomatic, military, economic and cultural efforts.

Thus, while geopolitics deals with the influence of geography on politics and international relations, international politics deals with international relations and their influence on politics. Global political strategy deals with planning and implementing specific actions to achieve political goals at the international level.

LET'S START THE JOURNEY

IN THE FOLLOWING PAGES, WE WILL GIVE SOME EXAMPLES OF PROCEEDING WITH THE RESEARCH AND ANALYSIS OF GEOPOLITICS AS WELL AS INTERNATIONAL POLITICS AND INTERNATIONAL POLICY STRATEGY.

We are not talking about exhaustive but synthetic analyses, as they are complex and constantly evolving topics.

In fact, many experts may have different opinions on how geopolitical situations will become in the future because, as we will see, many variables are determined by internal political choices that impact international political strategies.

Still, also climate variables (natural disasters, for example) and technological progress can determine new choices.

We will take a trip worldwide by reading these geopolitical overviews, focusing on some relevant aspects. To give you an example of acquiring and processing information to know and evaluate.

Let's start the journey!

PART TWO

HOW DO YOU ANALYZE GEOPOLITICS, INTERNATIONAL POLITICS AND INTERNATIONAL POLITICAL STRATEGY?

Taking the United States as an example, one would analyze how its geographical location, such as its access to the sea and its borders with Canada and Mexico, affects its politics and international relations. In addition, one would examine how the United State's natural resources, such as oil, gas, and coal, impact its economy and industry.

We would study how geographical factors, such as climate and terrain, influence the historical development of the United States and its politics.

About American international policy: we would analyze how the United States interacts with other nations and international organizations, such as the United Nations. We would study how the United States influences international politics through diplomatic relations, trade, and development aid.

Finally, we will examine how the United States uses their position as a world superpower to influence international politics.

It is concluded that geography affects the United States' politics and international relations. In contrast, American international policy deals with how the United States influences international politics and interacts with other nations and international organizations.

American political strategy is how the United States plans and implements specific actions to achieve international political objectives.

That's correct. American political strategy can include diplomatic, military, economic, and cultural actions.

The United States, as a global superpower, has a wide range of interests on the international stage. Their international political strategy aims to protect and promote these interests through various actions.

For example, the United States has a robust military presence in various parts of the world, such as the Middle East and Asia, to protect strategic interests and ensure national security.

Additionally, the United States has diplomatic relations with many other countries and participates in international organizations such as the United Nations to promote peace and stability globally.

It is also important to note that American political strategy is influenced by the current government's priorities and the evolving international circumstances. These factors can result in shifts in the strategy over time.

 The method described is one of several ways to begin understanding and utilizing geopolitics. Let's apply this method and start our journey into global geopolitics. Remember that these are not exhaustive examples, but they should be sufficient to create a good understanding of geopolitical events from 2000 to 2021.

Let's begin!

PART THREE

UNITED STATES OF AMERICA

THE GEOPOLITICS, INTERNATIONAL POLITICS, AND INTERNATIONAL POLITICAL STRATEGY OF THE UNITED STATES IN THE LAST TWO DECADES (2000-2021)

The United States' geopolitics in the last two decades has been influenced mainly by the country's geographical location, its natural resources, borders, and other geographical factors. For example, United States geopolitics has been influenced by the increasing importance of fossil fuels and renewable energy in the United States and the need to protect the United State's natural resources.

United States geopolitics has also been influenced by the growing concern over climate change and the need to take measures to combat it.

The United States' international politics in the last two decades have been influenced by the country's relations with other nations and international organizations. For example, the United States' international politics has been influenced by its relations with NATO and other Western allies and its relations with emerging countries such as China and India. In addition, the United States' international politics has been influenced by the decision to withdraw military troops from certain conflict zones such as Iraq and Afghanistan.

The United States' international political strategy in the last two decades has been influenced by the need to achieve international political objectives. For example, the United States international political strategy has been influenced by the decision to send military troops to conflict zones to protect the United States' strategic interests or by using economical aid to promote stability in developing countries.

The United States' international political strategy has also been influenced by the growing concern over climate change and the need to protect the United State's natural resources.

In the last two decades, many factors have influenced the United States' geopolitics, international politics, and international political strategy.

Some of these factors include:

Political changes: The United States has experienced significant political changes in the last two decades, including transitioning from a Democratic to a Republican party government and vice versa. These changes have impacted the United States' geopolitics and international politics.

* ❖ **Economic crisis:** The United States went through a severe economic crisis starting in 2008, followed by economic growth. These economic developments have impacted the United States' geopolitics and international politics.

* ❖ **Relations with the European Union and Russia:** The United States' relations with the European Union and Russia have often been complex and have significantly impacted the United States' geopolitics and international politics. For example, tensions with Russia after the annexation of Crimea in 2014 led to the imposition of economic sanctions by the United States.

* ❖ **Military interventions:** The United States has conducted military interventions in various parts of the world in the last two decades, such as in Afghanistan and Iraq. These interventions have impacted the United States' geopolitics and international politics.

❖ **Global challenges:** The United States has faced various global challenges in the last two decades, such as climate change and the threat of international terrorism, which have influenced its geopolitics and international politics.

SUMMARY OF THE KEY MILESTONES OF UNITED STATES INTERNATIONAL POLICY AND POLITICAL STRATEGY 2000-2021

Here is a non-exhaustive list of key milestones of the United States' international policy and political strategy from 2000 to 2021:

- 2000: The election of George W. Bush as president of the United States marks a significant shift in U.S. foreign policy, with an increased emphasis on national defence and security.

- 2001: September 11 attacks. The United States responded with Operation Enduring Freedom in Afghanistan and Operation Iraqi Freedom in Iraq.

- 2002: NATO expands the area of operations of the Bosnia and Herzegovina Stabilisation Mission (SFOR) to the whole of Bosnia and Herzegovina.

- 2003: The United States invades Iraq to disarm Saddam Hussein's regime and find and destroy weapons of mass destruction that the regime was accused of possessing.

- 2004: The U.S. government launches the "War on Terror," a global campaign against terrorism.

- 2005: The United States and Canada introduce economic sanctions against Iran for its nuclear program.

- 2006: Iran and the negotiating group known as the P5+1 (United States, United Kingdom, France, Russia, China, and Germany) begin negotiating the Iran nuclear deal.

- 2002: NATO expands the area of operations of the Bosnia and Herzegovina Stabilization Mission (SFOR) to the whole of Bosnia and Herzegovina.

- 2003: The United States invades Iraq to disarm Saddam Hussein's regime and find and destroy weapons of mass destruction that the regime was accused of possessing.

- 2004: The U.S. government launches the "War on Terror," a global campaign against terrorism.

- 2005: The United States and Canada introduce economic sanctions against Iran for its nuclear program.

- 2006: Iran and the negotiating group known as the P5+1 (United States, United Kingdom, France, Russia, China, and Germany) begin negotiating the Iran nuclear deal.

- 2007: The United States begins withdrawing troops from Iraq.

- 2008: The election of Barack Obama as President of the United States marks a significant shift in U.S. foreign policy, with an increased emphasis on diplomacy and international cooperation.

- 2009: The United States begins withdrawing troops from Afghanistan.

- 2010: Iran and the P5+1 temporarily agree on Iran's nuclear program, known as the Geneva Accord.

- 2011: The United States participated in the international coalition that imposed a no-fly zone in Libya, leading to the fall of Muammar Gaddafi's regime.

- 2012: The United States agreed with Afghanistan to hand security responsibilities to the Afghan government.

- 2013: The United States and Russia agreed to destroy Syrian chemical weapons.

- 2014: The civil war in Syria began, and US military intervention against the Islamic State.

- 2014: ISIS emerged as a significant threat in Iraq and Syria, and the United States began conducting airstrikes against ISIS positions.

- 2015: The United States and the P5+1 reached a final agreement on Iran's nuclear program, known as the Vienna Agreement.

- 2016: The election of Donald Trump as President of the United States marks a significant shift in U.S. foreign policy, with an increased emphasis on protecting national borders and defending domestic industries.

- 2017: The United States withdraws its membership in the Iran nuclear deal and reimposes economic sanctions against Iran.

- 2018: The United States and North Korea begin negotiating the denuclearization of the Korean peninsula. The historic meeting between President Trump and North Korean leader Kim Jong-un in Singapore.

- 2019: The US imposes trade tariffs on China and starts a trade war.

- 2020: Election of Joe Biden as President of the United States.

- 2020: The United States is affected by the COVID-19 pandemic, which has significantly impacted international politics and U.S. political strategy.

- 2021: The United States reaches a peace agreement with Afghanistan, which provides for the withdrawal of US troops.

- 2021: The United States struggles with the COVID-19 pandemic and grapples with tensions with Iran, China, and other nations. In addition, the country has been hit by unprecedented political and social events, including the storming of the US Capitol on January 6, 2021.

The United States is currently facing a series of internal challenges. Some of the most relevant internal issues that the United States may face could include the following:

• Combatting economic and social inequality, which can lead to tensions within society and undermine national cohesion

• Managing issues of racial justice and gender equality, as the United States still has a long way to go to ensure equality for all citizens

• Managing the COVID-19 pandemic and its implications for health, the economy, and society

• Managing demographic changes and cultural diversity within the country

• Protecting the environment and managing natural resources sustainably

• Managing international conflicts and national security, particularly the fight against terrorism and the proliferation of weapons of mass destruction

• Managing financial crisis and economic recession

• Managing immigration issues and asylum policies

• Reforming the healthcare system and healthcare policies

• Reforming the justice system

• Managing demographic changes and cultural diversity within the country

• Protecting the environment and managing natural resources sustainably

• Managing relations with rising powers such as China and maintaining the United States' global leadership

• Managing climate change and its implications for

United States interests

****

POVERTY IS A SIGNIFICANT ISSUE IN THE UNITED STATES. ACCORDING TO THE UNITED STATES CENSUS BUREAU, ABOUT 10.7% OF THE U.S. POPULATION LIVED IN POVERTY IN 2020.

There have been many efforts to address poverty in the United States, but the problem persists.

Some causes of poverty in the United States include the rising cost of living, low minimum wage, lack of access to basic services such as healthcare and education, and discrimination based on race, gender, and sexual orientation.

Additionally, some specific population groups like children, the elderly, the disabled, minorities, and single-parent households have a higher risk of poverty, and programs or policies to support those populations still need improvement.

THE DEFENCE SPENDING BUDGET OF THE UNITED STATES is very high and represents a significant portion of the federal funding. In 2020, the United States defence spending budget was around $740 billion, representing about 15% of the federal budget. This means that a significant portion of the government's financial resources is allocated to defence, leaving fewer resources available for other priorities such as education, health, and poverty.

Opinions of Americans on the United States military aggression policy can vary greatly. Moreover, their political views can also influence Americans' opinions on the United States' military aggression policy. For example, Americans who identify as conservatives often support a strong defence policy. In contrast, those identifying as progressives tend to be more critical of the United States military aggression policy.

But what is the United States' geopolitical strategy?

The United States has a unique global position of power as the world's largest economy and a military superpower. Their geopolitical strategy aims to maintain this leadership position and protect their national interests worldwide. Many factors influence their strategy, including security, economy, trade, energy, international relations, and domestic policies.

The United States has several military and political alliances worldwide, including the North Atlantic Treaty Organization (NATO) and the Partnership for Peace Agreement (PPA). They also work closely with other economic powers like the European Union and Japan to promote peace and stability at an international level.

The United States is also committed to protecting its economic interests through international trade and trade agreements, such as the Trans-Pacific Partnership (TPP) and the North American Free Trade Agreement (NAFTA). They also seek to promote access to safe, affordable energy sources to support their economy.

Additionally, the United States has a history of military intervention in various parts of the world to protect its national interests and promote peace and stability. However, this strategy is often controversial and can negatively affect the international scene.

The United States' geopolitical strategy generally aims to maintain its global leadership position and protect its national interests through alliances, trade, energy, and military intervention if necessary.

****

NATO

The North Atlantic Treaty Organization (NATO) was founded in 1949 to protect Western Europe from military threats from the Soviet Union during the Cold War.

After the dissolution of the Soviet Union in 1991, NATO has continued to exist. However, it has taken on several new challenges, including the fight against terrorism and violent extremism.

The United States and many other members of NATO believe the alliance is still vital for security and stability in Europe and the North Atlantic.

NATO provides a platform for military and political cooperation among its members and plays a vital role in promoting peace and stability at an international level.

However, the existence of NATO has been debated in some countries, particularly those that were part of the Soviet Union or had complex relations with the alliance in the past.

Some argue that NATO should be dissolved or have a reduced role in international security. In contrast, others believe the alliance is still important for European security and stability.

For example, Russia has expressed concern about expanding NATO to the east, arguing that it could threaten national security.

However, some European countries have expressed concern about NATO's role or desire to increase their autonomy in defence matters on different occasions in recent years.

For example, France has expressed a desire to increase its autonomy in defence matters and reduce its involvement with NATO in some military operations. In 1966, France left NATO's integrated military structure and withdrew the rest of its forces from NATO. However, it remained a member of the alliance and continued participating in various military operations under NATO command.

Other European countries, such as Germany, Italy, and the United Kingdom, have also expressed a desire to increase their autonomy in defence matters or reduce their involvement with NATO in some military operations in the past.

These countries remain alliance members, participating in various military operations under NATO command.

In general, while some NATO member countries have expressed a desire to increase their autonomy in defence matters or reduce their involvement with the alliance in some military operations, most member countries believe that NATO is still important for security and stability in Europe and the North Atlantic.

However, its role and future may be subject to debate.

GREAT BRITAIN

BRITISH GEOPOLITICS, INTERNATIONAL POLITICS AND INTERNATIONAL POLITICAL STRATEGY OVER THE PAST TWENTY YEARS.

Over the past twenty years, British geopolitics has mainly been influenced by the UK's geographical location, natural resources, borders, and other factors.

For example, British geopolitics was influenced by the UK's decision to leave the European Union, also known as Brexit, which significantly impacted the UK's geographical position vis-à-vis the EU and continental Europe.

British geopolitics has been influenced by growing concern about climate change and the need to protect the UK's natural resources.

 Over the past twenty years, British international politics has been influenced by the UK's international relations with other nations and international organizations.

For example, British international politics has been influenced by the UK's decision to leave the European Union and the consequences of this decision on the UK's position internationally.

The UK's relations with the US and other NATO nations have influenced British international politics.

British international **political strategy** over the past twenty years has been influenced by the need to achieve political goals at the international level.

For example, British international political strategy has been influenced by the UK's decision to send military troops to conflict zones to protect the UK's strategic interests or by using economical aid to promote stability in developing countries.

Britain's international political strategy has been influenced by growing concern about climate change and the need to protect the UK's natural resources.

Influence of the Commonwealth

The Commonwealth administration is an intergovernmental organization of 54 countries, many of which are former British colonies.

The administration of the Commonwealth aims to promote cooperation and development among its members through sharing knowledge, experience and resources.

Over the past twenty years, British geopolitics, international politics and political strategy have been influenced by many factors, including relations with members of the Commonwealth, relations with the European Union and other nations and international organizations, and security and defiance issues.

For example, British geopolitics has been influenced by the importance of trade with Commonwealth countries and the need to protect the natural resources of the United Kingdom and its overseas territories.

British international politics has been influenced by relations with the European Union, the United States and other nations and international organizations, as well as the need to protect the strategic interests of the United Kingdom.

Finally, British international political strategy has been influenced by the need to achieve political objectives at the international level, such as promoting stability and peace in the world.

Britain has faced and will continue to face many challenges within and within the Commonwealth.

Many Commonwealth countries were British colonies and suffered the consequences of slavery and British imperialism.

Britain has faced demands for reparations for injustices suffered during slavery. It has sought to strengthen ties with Commonwealth countries through trade and cooperation.

Brexit and the European Union

 Brexit, the UK's decision to leave the European Union, has significantly impacted the European Union's geopolitics, international politics and international political strategy.

In terms of geopolitics, Brexit has resulted in a reduction in natural resources and the surface area of the European Union, as well as the loss of one of its leading members.

Brexit impacted the European Union's geographical position, as the United Kingdom was an essential bridge to the Commonwealth.

Regarding international politics, Brexit has impacted the relationship between the European Union and the United Kingdom, which has become less close. In addition, Brexit affected the European Union's relationship with the United States, as the United Kingdom was an essential ally of the West and a trading partner of the European Union.

Regarding international political strategy, Brexit has resulted in a shift in the European Union's strategy to achieve political goals internationally.

For example, the European Union had to find new ways to promote stability and peace in developing countries, as the United Kingdom was no longer a member of the European Union.

In addition, the European Union had to find new strategies to protect the economic and commercial interests of the European Union internationally since the United Kingdom was no longer a member of the European Union.

I hope this gives you more details about the geopolitics, international politics and international political strategy of the European Union over the past twenty years, both before and after Brexit.

In 2021 Britain was still a member of the EU and had just completed the process of leaving the Union, known as Brexit, on January 31, 2020. However, during the transition period, which lasted until 31 December 2020, Britain continued participating in EU policies and activities as a full member. Still, it no longer had representation in the Union's decision-making process.

Brexit has been a complex process, raising several challenges for Britain internally and within the Commonwealth.

Domestically, one of the biggest challenges for Britain has been managing the economic and trade implications of leaving the EU. Britain was the EU's leading trading partner, and leaving the Union meant the end of the free movement of goods, services and people between the UK and the EU. This has increased costs for businesses operating in both regions and has raised concerns about the impact on the UK economy.

Britain faced the challenge of maintaining positive and cooperative relations with EU countries, many of which are also members of the Commonwealth (Cyprus, Malta and Ireland). Accordingly, Britain has sought to negotiate trade and cooperation agreements with the EU and has worked to promote stability and security in Europe.

Within the Commonwealth, Brexit has impacted Britain's relationship with Commonwealth countries. In the past, many Commonwealth countries have had strong trade and cultural ties with Britain as former British colonies. However, after Brexit, Britain had to negotiate new trade agreements with these countries and maintain good relations with them.

Other challenges for the UK

Domestically, one of the biggest challenges for Britain is rising economic and social inequalities. Significant income and opportunity gaps exist between different regions of the country and different sections of the population.

In addition, Britain is facing some demographic challenges, such as an ageing population and population decline in some areas of the country.

Other domestic challenges for Britain include protecting the environment, increasing chronic diseases such as diabetes and cardiovascular disease, and improving public services, such as education and the health system.

According to some geopolitical experts, one of the biggest challenges for Britain geopolitically is its role in a rapidly changing world where new economic and political powers are emerging.

Britain has traditionally enjoyed a leading position globally, both as a member of the EU and as a member of NATO.

However, with Brexit and the change in the distribution of global power, Britain may be in a weaker position in the future.

Britain faces the challenge of maintaining good relations with its key allies, such as the United States and working with them to address common challenges, such as climate change and international security.

However, Britain must also manage its relations with the EU and other countries in a way that protects its economic and political interests.

EUROPEAN UNION

EUROPEAN UNION

The analysis of the European Union member countries' 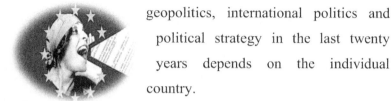 geopolitics, international politics and political strategy in the last twenty years depends on the individual country.

Over the past twenty years, the European Union and its member countries have faced several geopolitical, international and strategic challenges.

Regarding geopolitics, member countries' geographical locations and natural resources have continued to affect their geopolitics. In addition, the European Union has been influenced by geopolitical dynamics globally, such as the growing influence of China and Russia.

Regarding international politics, the European Union and its member countries have maintained positive relations with other world powers, such as the United States and Japan. However, they have also faced challenges managing relations with Mediterranean countries and the European Union. In addition, the European Union has also had to deal with issues related to international security, such as terrorism and migration.

In terms of international political strategy, the member countries of the European Union have adopted different strategies to achieve political goals at the international level.

For example, some countries have adopted a strategy of dialogue and cooperation with the countries of the southern Mediterranean to promote stability and peace in the region. In contrast, others have adopted a strategy of neutrality. The European Union has also worked to promote a standard security policy and to strengthen its position as a global actor.

SOME EXAMPLES OF HOW THESE FACTORS HAVE INFLUENCED THE GEOPOLITICS, INTERNATIONAL POLITICS AND INTERNATIONAL POLITICAL STRATEGY OF THE MEMBER COUNTRIES OF THE EUROPEAN UNION IN THE LAST TWENTY YEARS:

1. **Economic and financial crisis: The global economic and financial** crisis of 2008 significantly impacted EU economic policy, including financial aid and rescue measures for some member countries in difficulty.

2. **Demographic changes:** Demographic changes, such as the rapid ageing of the population in some EU countries, have impacted EU social policy and the strategy to address these demographic challenges.

3.   **Migration and refugees:** The refugee crisis in Europe has had a significant impact on EU asylum and immigration policy, including how the EU manages refugee flows and how it protects refugee rights.

4.   **Development of the Economic and Monetary Union:** The adoption of the euro as the single currency by many EU countries has had a significant impact on the EU's monetary policy and the economic stability of the euro area, although, in my view, very controversial.

5.   **Relations with third countries:** The EU's relations with third countries, such as the United States and Russia, have continued to evolve and influence the EU's foreign policy. For example, tensions with Russia after the annexation of Crimea in 2014 led to the adoption of economic sanctions by the EU.

6.   **Global challenges:** Global challenges like climate change have affected the EU's environmental policy and strategy to address this global challenge. The threat of international terrorism has led to the adoption of security measures by the EU to protect EU citizens.

DOES THE EUROPEAN UNION HAVE ITS OWN GEOPOLITICS?

Yes, the European Union (EU) has its own geopolitics. Geopolitics is the analysis of the interactions between political, economic, and social forces and the geographical features of a region. In this sense, the EU has its own geopolitics since it is a political and economic entity that acts in a given geographical area and interacts with this region's political, economic and social forces.

The EU also has its own Common Foreign and Security Policy (CFSP), which is responsible for defining and conducting the EU's foreign and security policy. The CFSP is an essential component of the EU's geopolitics. It encompasses several areas, such as relations with third countries, international cooperation and crisis management.

In addition, the EU is a global player and plays an important role on the international scene in several areas, such as trade, environment, security and international cooperation. This is all part of the EU's geopolitics and influences the EU's relations with other global players.

SUMMARY OF THE MILESTONES OF THE LAST TWENTY YEARS OF INTERNATIONAL POLITICS AND POLITICAL STRATEGY OF THE EUROPEAN UNION:

1.   2000: Many EU countries adopted the euro as a single currency.

2.   2004: Enlargement of the EU to 10 new countries, bringing the total number of member countries to 25.

3.   2007: Signing the Lisbon Treaty, which reforms the EU's institutional structure and strengthens its Common Foreign and Security Policy (CFSP).

4.   2008: The beginning of the global financial and economic crisis, which significantly impacted EU economic policy.

5.   2010: Adoption of the EU's neighbourhood policy, which aims to strengthen relations with the countries of Eastern Europe, the Caucasus and the Mediterranean.

6.   2014: The annexation of Crimea by Russia and the start of the conflict in Ukraine had a significant impact on EU foreign policy and led to the adoption of economic sanctions by the EU.

7.   2015: Start of the refugee crisis in Europe, which raised complex issues related to international law and international solidarity and significantly impacted EU asylum and immigration policy.

8.   2016: Brexit, the UK's vote to leave the EU, significantly impacted the EU's geopolitics and international politics.

9.   2020: Start of the COVID-19 pandemic, which has significantly impacted the EU's geopolitics and international politics and raised issues related to international cooperation and solidarity.

Geopolitical experts agree that the EU faces several domestic and international geopolitical challenges.

Internally, the EU faces the risk of divisions within the Union, particularly with Brexit and the possible strengthening of separatist movements in some countries.

In addition, the rising wave of immigration from developing countries and the increase in the Muslim population in some parts of the EU have raised concerns about internal cohesion and security.

The COVID-19 pandemic has had a significant impact on the EU's geopolitics. It has exposed the Union's weaknesses and raised questions about its ability to deal with global crises.

The geopolitics of the European Union is a complex and ever-evolving topic. Consequently, experts may have different views on how the EU's geopolitical situation will evolve.

HOWEVER, SOME TRENDS COULD AFFECT THE GEOPOLITICS OF THE EU IN THE FUTURE:

Increasing the EU's economic power: The EU is the largest economy in the world and is constantly growing. This could increase its geopolitical weight worldwide.

Increasing international cooperation: The EU is an important player in the international system and has close ties with many countries worldwide. International cooperation could increase in the future, giving the EU an even more influential role at a global level.

China's growing influence: China is becoming increasingly powerful economically and militarily, which could impact the EU's geopolitics. For example, the EU may face competition from China in international markets or may need to consider Chinese influence in security matters.

Political uncertainty: The EU faces domestic challenges, such as Brexit and political tensions in some member countries. These political uncertainties could have an impact on the EU's geopolitics in the future.

Developments in other parts of the world: Developments in other parts, such as political tensions or economic crises, could impact the geopolitics of the EU.

For example, tensions with a country important to the EU could affect its geopolitical position.

Many factors could represent internal problems for the European Union.

Here are some of the challenges the EU may face:

Economic and social inequalities: There are strong economic and social inequalities within the EU, with some countries thriving and others struggling. These inequalities could cause tensions within the EU and put the cohesion of the Union at risk.

Brexit: The UK voted to leave the EU in 2016, and the Brexit process was complex and controversial. The UK's exit from the EU represents a challenge for the EU. It could impact its unity and ability to act globally.

Political tensions: There have been some political tensions within  the EU, such as the case of Hungary and Poland, which have raised concerns about human rights and democracy in the EU. Such tensions could undermine the cohesion of the Union and its ability to act coherently.

Economic crisis: The EU has faced a severe economic crisis since 2008, and some member countries still have difficulty recovering. The economic crisis could continue challenging the EU and undermining citizens' trust in the Union.

Migration: The EU has faced a wave of migrants and refugees in recent years, which has raised concerns about security and cohesion within the EU. Finding a way to effectively manage migration could be challenging for the EU.

To address these challenges, experts believe the EU needs to strengthen its internal cohesion and global power by adopting greater diplomacy and common defence capability.

The EU must find ways to cooperate with other global powers, such as the US and China, to address global challenges effectively.

Eurozone crisis

The eurozone crisis is an economic and financial crisis that has hit the European Union since 2008. The crisis began with the collapse of the housing market in the United States. Then, it spread to Europe, hitting some eurozone countries hard, such as Greece, Ireland, Portugal, Italy and Spain.

The eurozone crisis was caused by several factors, including:

- High economic and social inequalities within the eurozone
- High public debts in some eurozone countries
- High dependence on foreign loans in some eurozone countries
- Lack of a debt-sharing mechanism within the eurozone

The eurozone crisis has had serious economic and social consequences for the countries involved, such as rising unemployment, reduced purchasing power and increasing social tensions.

The EU and the ECB have taken several measures to deal with the crisis, such as the eurozone bailout programme and the ECB's quantitative easing policy. However, the eurozone crisis is still a major challenge for the EU.

****

P.I.G.S.

The PIGS is an acronym for some eurozone countries that have been hit hard by the economic and financial crisis since 2008. The acronym PIGS refers to Portugal, Italy, Greece and Spain.

During the eurozone crisis, GDPs faced problems such as high public debt, high unemployment and economic recession. To address these problems, the P.I.G.S. had to undertake difficult reforms, such as cutting wages and social benefits and received loans from the EU and the IMF to help them cope with the crisis.

During the eurozone crisis, these countries faced financial problems and were the subject of concern from financial markets.

As a result, they have also come under intense pressure from the EU and the ECB to implement economic and financial reforms to bring their public deficits under control.

These measures include:

EUROZONE BAILOUT PROGRAMME: The EU and IMF have provided loans to eurozone countries, including GDPs, to help them cope with the crisis. **However, these loans have been conditional on countries' commitment to undertake difficult reforms, such as cutting wages and social benefits.**

ECB LEASING QUANTITY: The ECB has launched a government bond purchase programme, known as leasing quantity, to increase liquidity in the eurozone and support economic growth.

STRUCTURAL REFORMS: The EU and ECB have urged eurozone countries, including GDPs, to undertake structural reforms to increase competitiveness and long-term growth. Such reforms may have included the reduction of trade barriers, the liberalisation of markets and the cutting of public spending for some of these countries.

The EU'S INTERNAL POLICY towards GDPs during the eurozone crisis was aimed at supporting these countries through loans and other support measures but also at encouraging structural reforms to ensure the long-term sustainability of the economy.

These measures have often been controversial. They have raised concerns about the effects of GDPs on citizens, such as rising unemployment and reduced social benefits.

However, using the acronym PIGS to refer to these countries has often been considered offensive and discriminatory, as it suggests that these countries are inferior to other EU countries. Therefore, the acronym PIGS is often avoided and is no longer widely used.

At the end of 2021, the situation of the EU and the GPS WAS STILL MARKED BY THE CONSEQUENCES OF THE EUROZONE CRISIS. Although the EU had experienced economic growth in recent years, some countries, notably GDPs, still struggled to recover from the crisis.

Especially:

Greece: Greece has been one of the countries hardest hit by the eurozone crisis and has had to undertake difficult reforms to receive loans from the EU and IMF. Despite some progress, Greece still has a high unemployment rate and public debt.

Portugal: Portugal faced similar difficulties to Greece during the eurozone crisis but has experienced solid economic growth in recent years. However, the high unemployment rate and public debt remain a concern.

Spain: Spain has also been hit hard by the eurozone crisis but has experienced solid economic growth recently. However, the unemployment rate is still relatively high, and there are concerns about public debt.

Italy: Italy has also been hit by the eurozone crisis but has experienced weak economic growth recently. Public debt is a significant concern for Italy, and there are concerns about the long-term sustainability of the economy.

In general, the EU and GDP at the end of 2021 were still affected by the consequences of the eurozone crisis. However, some progress has been made in coping with the crisis.

RUSSIA

GEOPOLITICS, INTERNATIONAL POLITICS AND INTERNATIONAL POLITICAL STRATEGY RUSSIA IN THE LAST TWENTY YEARS.

Russia's strong history and unique geographical position have influenced its development and relationship with other countries. Russia is the largest country in the world by area, and its territory stretches from Western Europe to East Asia.

Its geographical position makes it an important geopolitical player internationally.

IN RECENT YEARS, RUSSIA HAS ADOPTED A STRATEGY OF "RAPPROCHEMENT" WITH THE COUNTRIES OF THE FORMER SOVIET BLOC AND SOUGHT TO STRENGTHEN ITS TIES WITH EASTERN EUROPE AND CENTRAL ASIA. IT HAS ALSO SOUGHT TO EXPAND ITS MILITARY PRESENCE IN DIFFERENT PARTS OF THE WORLD, SUCH AS THE MIDDLE EAST AND AFRICA.

Russia's most relevant geopolitical aspects are related to its unique geographical position, which makes it a bridge between Europe and Asia.

This has led to some of the region's most important geopolitical issues, such as the war in Afghanistan and energy security issues.

Russia is also ONE OF THE WORLD'S LEADING NUCLEAR POWERS, WITH AN ARSENAL OF ABOUT **4,300** WARHEADS, which confers considerable deterrence power and influence on the international stage.

Russia is also ONE OF THE WORLD'S LEADING ENERGY PRODUCERS, WITH VAST OIL AND NATURAL GAS DEPOSITS. This has given it a leading position in supplying energy to many Eastern Europe and Central Asia countries.

Russia also has a significant presence in other regions, such as the Middle East and Africa, where it has economic and strategic interests.

Many factors have influenced Russia's geopolitics, international politics and political strategy over the past twenty years.

Some of these factors include:

Political changes: Russia has experienced significant political changes over the past two decades, including transitioning from a mixed economy to a market economy system and Vladimir Putin's return to power as president in 2012. These changes have had an impact on Russia's geopolitics and international politics.

Economic crisis: Russia went through a severe economic crisis in the 1990s, followed by a period of economic growth during Putin's rule starting in 2000. These economic developments have impacted Russia's geopolitics and international politics.

Relations with the European Union and the United States: Russia's relations with the European Union and the United States have often been complex and have significantly impacted Russia's geopolitics and international politics.

Russia has also sought to strengthen its position in the region of the former Soviet Union through the Eurasian Economic Union and other regional integration initiatives. However, his attempt to annex Crimea in 2014 and his involvement in the insurgency in eastern Ukraine led to a deterioration of relations with the West and a series of economic sanctions, especially by the EU.

Military interventions: Russia has conducted military interventions in different parts of the world over the past two decades, such as Georgia in 2008 and Ukraine in 2014. These interventions have had an impact on Russia's geopolitics and international politics.

Global challenges: Russia has faced several global challenges over the past two decades, such as climate change and the threat of international terrorism, affecting its geopolitics and international politics.

Russia has several military allies and economic partners around the world. Its main military allies are *China, Kazakhstan, Kyrgyzstan, Tajikistan and Turkmenistan,* which are part of the SHANGHAI COOPERATION ORGANIZATION (SCO), an international organization for regional cooperation founded in Central Asia. In addition, it has bilateral military alliances with several countries, including China, India and Vietnam.

Russia also has a defence agreement with India. It has developed **military relations with Iran, Venezuela and Syria**.

Russia is a member of the COLLECTIVE SECURITY TREATY ORGANIZATION (CSTO), a military alliance that includes Armenia, Belarus, Kazakhstan, Kyrgyzstan and Tajikistan.

Russia's international politics and political strategy over the past two decades have been characterized by an attempt to restore its position as a global power through the modernization of its armed forces and involvement in international issues such as the war in Syria and relations with the United States.

Russia has also sought to strengthen its relations with the countries of the former Soviet bloc through the Eurasian Economic Union and other initiatives. However, as they have already mentioned, his attempt to annex Crimea in 2014 and his involvement in the insurgency in eastern Ukraine have led to a deterioration of relations with the West and a series of economic sanctions.

Russia has also adopted a strategy of **"MULTIVECTORIALITY"** in its relations with other countries, trying to develop positive relations with all major world powers and avoid depending too much on a single partner. This allowed it to maintain flexibility and not be too tied to a specific political or economic bloc.

Russia has also sought to promote **MULTILATERALISM** and respect for the rules of international law through its involvement in organizations such as the UN and the UN Security Council and through the adoption of initiatives such as the Treaty on the Prohibition of Nuclear Weapons.

Russia has also adopted a "BALANCE OF POWER" strategy in many of its international relations, seeking to maintain a level playing field with the other major world powers and not to depend on a single source of alliances or resources.

Russia's international politics has been characterized by challenges and opportunities over the past twenty years. Russia has sought to strengthen its position as a global power and defend its strategic interests in the region and internationally.

During this time, Russia faced several challenges, including the US meddling in key regions, such as Eastern Europe and the Middle East, and tensions with some European Union and NATO nations. RUSSIA HAS ALSO HAD TO DEAL WITH CHINA'S GROWING INFLUENCE AND INCREASED GLOBAL GEOPOLITICAL COMPETITION.

To address these challenges, Russia has adopted an international political strategy to defend its strategic interests and promote **GLOBAL MULTIPOLARITY**, which aims to reduce the influence of the United States and the European Union.

Russia has also sought to strengthen its ties with other emerging powers, such as China, India and Brazil, through initiatives such as the Shanghai Cooperation Organization and BRICS.

Over the past decade, **Russia has also sought to strengthen its position in the energy world by diversifying its energy sources and expanding its energy transport networks.** In addition, Russia has also sought to strengthen its ties with post-Soviet countries through initiatives such as the Eurasian Union and the Shanghai Cooperation Council.

Regarding economic and financial partnerships, Russia has developed close economic relations with many countries in Europe, Asia and Latin America.

Russia also has an economic partnership with the European Union through the Eastern Partnership, which aims to promote economic and political cooperation between Russia and the EU.

Russia has developed close economic relations with China through the BRICS, a group of emerging countries that includes Brazil, Russia, India, China and South Africa.

Russia has significant economic relations with other Central Asian countries, such as Kazakhstan and Uzbekistan.

Russia has sought to promote greater international cooperation on global security issues, such as climate change and the fight against terrorism.

HOWEVER, RUSSIA'S RELATIONS WITH SOME WESTERN COUNTRIES HAVE REMAINED STRAINED DUE TO ISSUES SUCH AS **THE CRISIS IN UKRAINE AND ALLEGATIONS OF INTERFERENCE IN US ELECTIONS.**

Summarized in chronological order the milestones of the last twenty years of international politics and Russia's political strategy:

1. 2000: Vladimir Putin becomes Russia's president and modernises the armed forces and reforms the economy.

2.	2002: Russia joins the NATO-Russia Council, creating a forum for dialogue and cooperation with the Western alliance.

1.	2004: Russia joins the Shanghai Cooperation Organization (SCO), a regional security and cooperation organization that includes China, Kazakhstan, Kyrgyzstan, Tajikistan and Uzbekistan.

2.	2008: Russia sends troops to Georgia in response to a conflict in the South Caucasus region. Relations with the West deteriorate as a result of the intervention.

3.	2010: Russia signs a strategic partnership agreement with China, establishing a closer alliance between the two countries.

4.	2014: Russia drowns Crimea and begins supporting the insurgency in eastern Ukraine, leading to further deterioration of relations with the West and a series of economic sanctions.

5.	2015: Russia intervenes in Syria in support of the government of Bashar al-Assad, becoming a key player in the Syrian civil war.

6.	2017: Russia signs a peace agreement with the United States to disarm North Korea.

7.	2018: Russia participates in the first UN Security Council meeting on the non-proliferation of biological weapons, marking a step forward in international cooperation on biological security.

1. 2019: Russia signs the Treaty on the Prohibition of Nuclear Weapons, becoming the first country to ratify it.

❖ 2020: Russia expands its military presence in Afghanistan to support the Afghan government in the fight against the Taliban.

PUTIN AND THE NEW MULTIPOLAR ORDER

The new emerging multipolar order that Putin spoke of refers to a world where different regional and global powers coexist and influence the international stage instead of being dominated by a single dominant superpower.

The idea of a new emerging multipolar order was put forward by Putin in his speech to the Federal Duma in 2007, in which he stressed the need for a multipolar world in which no single power dominates international affairs but in which different powers work together to address global challenges. It represents an alternative vision of how the world should be organized to the current unipolar order, in which the United States is the dominant superpower.

However, the idea of a new multipolar order is not new and has been debated for decades. In the past, some observers have argued that the world was evolving towards a multipolar order due to the decline in the influence of the great colonial powers and the emergence of new economic and political powers.

According to Putin, this **new order** should be based on **principles of multipolarity, multilateralism and respect for the rules of international law.** Moreover, it should include Russia as one of the world's leading powers.

He also stressed the importance of developing positive relations with other emerging powers, such as **China, India and Brazil,** which are seen as **the main protagonists of the new emerging multipolar order.**

THE NEW MULTIPOLAR ORDER DOES NOT OPPOSE A SPECIFIC ENEMY BUT RATHER REPRESENTS AN ALTERNATIVE VISION OF HOW INTERNATIONAL RELATIONS SHOULD BE ORGANIZED AND HOW GLOBAL CHALLENGES SHOULD BE ADDRESSED.

The goal of the new multipolar order **is to promote a greater balance of power between different powers and to encourage greater cooperation to address global challenges, such as climate change, terrorism and economic inequalities.**

Summarizing: the new multipolar order should be based on cooperation and peaceful conflict resolution. Furthermore, it should promote respect for the rules of international law and international norms. In addition, it should also provide for greater involvement of international organisations, such as the UN, in managing global issues.

However, everyone does not share this vision of the new multipolar order.

SOME OBSERVERS ARGUE THAT RUSSIA CANNOT PLAY A LEADERSHIP ROLE IN A MULTIPOLAR WORLD AND THAT ITS ATTEMPT TO PROMOTE THIS VISION IS PRIMARILY MOTIVATED BY COUNTERING WESTERN INFLUENCE. IN ADDITION, THERE ARE ALSO CONCERNS THAT A MULTIPOLAR WORLD COULD BE LESS STABLE, WITH MORE POSSIBILITIES FOR CONFLICT BETWEEN DIFFERENT POWERS.

Many thinkers and scholars have written about a new multipolar order and how it could be organized and function. These scholars include political scientists, economists, historians, and other academics who have analyzed an emerging multipolar world's potential impact and implications.

SOME EXAMPLES OF US THINKERS AND SCHOLARS WHO HAVE WRITTEN ABOUT THE IDEA OF A NEW MULTIPOLAR ORDER INCLUDE:

1.   **John Mearsheimer,** American political scientist and professor at the University of Illinois at Chicago.

2. **Alexander Wendt,** American political scientist and professor at Ohio University.

3. **Fareed Zakaria,** American journalist and writer.

SOME EXAMPLES OF CHINESE THINKERS AND SCHOLARS WHO HAVE WRITTEN ABOUT THE IDEA OF A NEW MULTIPOLAR ORDER INCLUDE:

1. **Wang Jisi, professor of** international studies at Peking University and president of the Academy of Social Sciences of China.

2. **Yuen Foong Khong,** Professor of International Studies at the University of Singapore.

SOME EXAMPLES OF INDIAN THINKERS AND SCHOLARS WHO HAVE WRITTEN ABOUT THE IDEA OF A NEW MULTIPOLAR ORDER INCLUDE:

1. **Kishore Mahbubani**, Singaporean academic and diplomat.

2. **Shashi Tharoor,** Indian writer and politician.

AND FINALLY, SOME EXAMPLES OF RUSSIAN THINKERS AND SCHOLARS WHO HAVE WRITTEN ON THE SUBJECT INCLUDE:

1. **Alexander Dynkin,** Russian academician and president of the Moscow Academy of Sciences

2. **Sergei Karaganov**, Russian academician and chairman of the Moscow Committee for International Affairs

3. **Fyodor Lukyanov,** Russian academic and editor-in-chief of Russia in Global Affairs magazine

4. **Ivan Timofeev**, Director of the Program for Russia and Eurasia at the Institute of International Affairs in Moscow

5. **Igor Ivanov,** former Russian Minister of Foreign Affairs and Chairman of the Moscow Council for International Affairs

6. **Sergei Lavrov,** current Russian Minister of Foreign Affairs

7. **Dimitri Trenin,** director of the Carnegie Moscow Center and Russian academician

MIDDLE EAST

GEOPOLITICS, INTERNATIONAL POLITICS AND INTERNATIONAL POLITICAL STRATEGY OF MIDDLE EASTERN COUNTRIES IN THE LAST TWENTY YEARS

The Middle East is a geographical region that includes several countries in the Arab and non-Arab world. Middle Eastern countries may vary depending on the definition used, but usually include:

1.	Afghanistan	9.	Kuwait	
2.	Saudi Arabia	10.	Lebanon	
3.	Bahrain	11.	Oman	
4.	Egypt	12.	Qatar	
5.	Iran	13.	Syria	
6.	Iraq	14.	United	Arab
7.	Israel		Emirates	
8.	Jordan	15.	Yemen	

Some definitions might also include the following:

1.	Armenia	4.	Georgia
2.	Azerbaijan	5.	Pakistan
3.	Cyprus	6.	Turkey

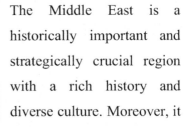

The Middle East is a historically important and strategically crucial region with a rich history and diverse culture. Moreover, it has an important role in international politics and world geopolitics because of its geographical location and natural resources, such as oil.

Over the past two decades, the geopolitics of the Middle East has been characterized by several changes and challenges.

One of the main factors influencing the international politics of Middle Eastern countries has been the conflict in Iraq and Afghanistan, which has had a significant impact on the region.

The issue of the State of Israel and the Palestinian territories has remained a source of tension in the Middle East, with numerous armed conflicts and peace negotiations taking place over the years.

The international political strategy of Middle **Eastern** countries has also been influenced by rising tensions with Iran, which has conducted a nuclear program and supported militant groups in different parts of the world.

In addition, the decline in oil reserves in the Middle East has impacted the political strategy of the region's countries since oil is an important source of income for many of them.

Other challenges that have influenced the geopolitics of the Middle East over the past two decades include climate change, population growth and the flow of migrants, as well as the rise of terrorism and religious extremism.

Countries in the Middle East have had to face these challenges and look for ways to solve or manage them effectively.

Some of the countries in the Middle East that have had greater geopolitical relevance in the last twenty years could be summarized:

Saudi Arabia: Saudi Arabia is one of the largest oil producers in the world and has a strategic geographical position in the region. It also has an important role in politics and the Islamic religion. In addition, it has a strong alliance with the United States.

Iran: Iran has a strong regional influence and a complex relationship with the West. It conducted a nuclear program and supported militant groups in different parts of the world, impacting its geopolitics and international politics.

Iraq: Iraq has a strategic geographical position and a rich history of cultures and influences. It also has significant oil reserves, which makes it an important geopolitical force. The war in Iraq and the conflict with ISIS have significantly impacted the region's geopolitics and international politics.

Israel: Israel has a strategic geographical position in the region and a long history of tensions with neighbouring Arab countries. It also has a strong alliance with the United States and an important role in international politics.

United Arab Emirates: The United Arab Emirates is a country with a strategic geographical position in the region and has a significant amount of oil reserves. They also sought to strengthen their relations with the West and adopt Western economic and political models.

Surely the last twenty years have been full of important events in international politics and the Middle East. *Here are some of the milestones that could be included in a summary:*

1. 2003: U.S. invasion of Iraq: The United States and a coalition of countries invaded Iraq to disable weapons of mass destruction believed to be Saddam Hussein's regime. The invasion led to a long and controversial war and increased tension and instability in the Middle East.

2. 2011: Arab Spring: A series of popular uprisings rocked North Africa and the Middle East, leading to the fall of several authoritarian regimes, including Muammar Gaddafi in Libya and Hosni Mubarak in Egypt.

1. 2014: Beginning of the civil war in Syria: The Syrian civil war, which is still ongoing, began as an uprising against President Bashar al-Assad, but soon became a complex conflict involving different factions and foreign powers. The war caused a major humanitarian crisis and gave rise to ISIS.

2.   2016: Election of Donald Trump as President of the United States: Trump's election led to a significant change in US policy and its relationship with the rest of the world, including the Middle East. He adopted a more overtly pro-Israel stance and withdrew the United States from the Iran nuclear deal.

3.   2020: Covid-19 pandemic: The Covid-19 pandemic has had a global impact on health, economics, politics, and the Middle East. It has also impacted conflict and crisis management in parts of the region.

Of course, many other important events could be mentioned. Still, these are some of the most significant of the last twenty years.

Middle East

FORMER SOVIET UNION COUNTRIES

1 Russia	6 Ukraine	11 Kazakhstan
2 Estonia	7 Moldova	12 Uzbekistan
3 Latvia	8 Georgia	13 Turkmenistan
4 Lithuania	9 Armenia	14 Kyrgystan
5 Belarus	10 Azerbaijan	15 Tajikistan

GEOPOLITICS, INTERNATIONAL POLITICS AND POLITICAL STRATEGY OF THE COUNTRIES OF THE FORMER SOVIET UNION IN THE LAST TWENTY YEARS EXCEPT FOR RUSSIA

The Soviet Union was a federal state comprising 15 independent Soviet republics, which dissolved with the dissolution of the USSR in 1991. The countries that identify with the definition of the former Soviet Union, except for Russia, are:

1.	Armenia	4.	Estonia
2.	Azerbaijan	5.	Georgia
3.	Belarus	6.	Kazakhstan

7.	Kyrgyzstan	11.	Tajikistan
8.	Latvia	12.	Turkmenistan
9.	Lithuania	13.	Ukraine
10.	Moldova	14.	Uzbekistan

All these countries became independent at the time of the dissolution of the USSR. As a result, they developed their own political and economic institutions.

The end of the Soviet Union and the dissolution of the USSR in 1991 had a significant impact on the geopolitics and international politics of the countries of the former Soviet Union, except for Russia.

Many of these countries sought to strengthen their relations with the West and adopt Western economic and political models. In contrast, others maintained closer relations with Russia and followed more authoritarian models.

The **international political strategy** of the countries of the former Soviet Union, except for Russia, has been influenced by different challenges and opportunities over the past twenty years.

For example, many of these countries have sought to integrate into the European Union and the Organization for Security and Cooperation in Europe (OSCE). Some of them have achieved EU membership or candidate status. Other countries have sought to strengthen their relations with the United States and Western countries.

The issue of territorial conflicts and ethnic minorities has been a source of tension in some countries of the former Soviet Union, except for Russia, such as Armenia, Azerbaijan, Georgia and Ukraine.

The situation in Ukraine, in particular, has had a significant impact on the geopolitics and international politics of the region, with the ongoing conflict between Ukraine and Russia and Russia's annexation of Crimea in 2014.

Other challenges that have influenced the geopolitics and international politics of the countries of the former Soviet Union, except for Russia, over the past two decades include the transition to a market economy, economic growth, climate change and terrorism.

The countries of the former Soviet Union, except for Russia, had to face these challenges and look for ways to solve or manage them effectively.

Some of the countries of the former Soviet Union, {except for Russia}, which has had greater geopolitical relevance in the last twenty years, could be summarized:

1. **Ukraine: The situation in Ukraine, particularly the ongoing conflict between Ukraine and Russia and Russia's annexation of Crimea in 2014, has significantly impacted the region's geopolitics and international politics**. Ukraine is also an important transportation corridor for European natural gas, making it an important geopolitical force.

2. **Georgia**: Georgia has a *strategic geographical position at the crossroads of Europe and Asia* and has sought to strengthen its relations with the West. It has also faced territorial conflicts with Azerbaijan and Russia, which has impacted its geopolitics and international politics.

3. **Armenia**: Armenia is a country that has had a long history of tensions with Azerbaijan due to an unresolved territorial conflict and an Armenian minority in Azerbaijan. It also had a complex relationship with Russia, which affected its geopolitics and international politics.

4. **Belarus**: Belarus has a ***strong relationship with Russia***, influencing its geopolitics and international politics. *However, it has also sought to strengthen its relations with the West and integrate into the European Union.*

1. **Kazakhstan**: Kazakhstan has a strategic *geographical position at the crossroads of Central Asia* and a rich history of cultures and influences. It also **has significant oil and gas reserves**, making it an important regional geopolitical force.

SUMMARY OF THE MAIN STAGES OF THE LAST TWENTY YEARS OF INTERNATIONAL POLITICS AND POLITICAL STRATEGY OF THE COUNTRIES OF THE FORMER SOVIET UNION, EXCEPT FOR RUSSIA:

1. 1991: Dissolution of the Soviet Union and the Commonwealth of Independent States (CIS) formation.

2. 1992: Signing the Lisbon Treaty establishing the Organization for Security and Co-operation in Europe (OSCE).

3.   1994: Ratification of the departure of all Russian troops from the Baltic.

4.   1995: Signing of the Budapest Treaty establishing the EU's Eastern Partnership with Armenia, Azerbaijan, Georgia, Moldova and Ukraine.

5.   2004: Accession of Estonia, Latvia and Lithuania to the EU and NATO.

6.   2014: Annexation of Crimea by Russia and the beginning of the conflict in Ukraine.

7.   2017: Ratification of the EU-Georgia Association Agreement and the EU-Moldova Association Agreement.

8.   2018: EU-Armenia Association Agreement signed.

9.   2019: EU-Azerbaijan Association Agreement signed.

INDO-ASIAN REGION

INDO-ASIAN GEOPOLITICS

The Indo-Asian area is a very large and diverse region, including many countries of great geopolitical importance. Here are some of the most important countries in the area:

India is the most populous country in the area and one of the major emerging economic powers. It has a strategic geographical position, is home to numerous international organizations and has a leadership role in the region.

China is the most populous country in the world and one of the world's largest economies. As a result, it greatly influences the Indo-Asian area economically and politically.

Japan: is one of the major economic powers in the world and has a strategic geographical position in the Pacific.

Indonesia: is the largest country in Southeast Asia and one of the most important economies in the region.

Philippines: They are one of the most dynamic economies in the region and have a strategic geographical position in the Pacific.

Pakistan is a country of great strategic importance since it borders Central Asia, South Asia and Western Asia.

Bangladesh: is one of the most densely populated countries in the world and one of the most dynamic emerging economies in the region.

Vietnam: is one of the most dynamic economies in South Asia and has a strategic geographical position in the Indo-Asian region.

THE INTERNATIONAL POLICY AND STRATEGY OF THE INDO-ASIAN COUNTRIES

The international policy and strategy of Indo-Asian countries vary widely from country to country. However, here is some information on the international policy and strategy of some of the Indo-Asian countries excluding India, Japan and China:

Philippines: The Philippines has a foreign policy promoting peace and security in South Asia. The Philippines is an ally of the United States and has close military cooperation with them. The Philippines is also a member of ASEAN and the UN.

Indonesia: Indonesia has a foreign policy based on neutrality and non-interference in the internal affairs of other countries. Indonesia is a member of the Association of Southeast Asian Nations (ASEAN) and has a leading position in the region.

Pakistan: Pakistan has a foreign policy based on national security and promoting peace and stability in the region. Pakistan has a complex relationship with the United States and close relations with China. Pakistan is a member of the UN and the Organization of Islamic Cooperation (OIC).

Bangladesh: Bangladesh has a foreign policy promoting peace and stability in the region. Bangladesh is a member of the UN and ASEAN.

Vietnam: Vietnam has a foreign policy promoting peace and stability in the Indo-Asian region. Vietnam is a member of **ASEAN** and **has close relations with China and the United States.**

THE GEOPOLITICAL SITUATION IN NORTHEAST ASIA

The countries of Northeast Asia are a geographical region that includes many countries in the northern part of East Asia. Some of the countries in Northeast Asia are:

1. China

2. Japan

3.   North Korea

4.   South Korea

5.   Taiwan

6.   Hong Kong

7.   Macau

This list may not be exhaustive, as the definition of "Northeast Asia" may vary depending on the context.

The geopolitical situation of Northeast Asia, except for China and Japan, is complex and constantly changing, as each country has unique challenges and opportunities and plays an important role in the region differently. However, some of the geopolitical issues that have impacted the region in recent years could be:

Tensions with South Korea: North Korea has had a complex relationship with South Korea and the United States. It faced the challenge of managing tensions with these countries and seeking a solution to the problem of nuclear proliferation.

Relations with China: North Korea has had a complex relationship with China, an important regional geopolitical force. He tried to maintain good relations with China but faced the challenge of managing tensions with that country.

Reluctance to adopt Western economic and political models: North Korea has sought to maintain a strongly planned and state-controlled economic and political system, in contrast to Western economic and political models. It faced the challenge of maintaining this system while trying to manage internal and external challenges.

The international **politics** and **political strategy of Northeast Asia countries, except China and Japan, have been influenced by the unique challenges and opportunities** each country has faced.

North Korea has adopted a strategy of nuclear development and proliferation of weapons of mass destruction to protect its regime and strengthen its international standing. It has also sought to maintain good relations with its neighbours and other important countries, such as China and Russia. Still, it has also faced tensions with the United States and South Korea.

North Korea, for example, has sought to maintain a strongly planned and state-controlled economic and political system, in contrast to Western economic and political models. It has also faced the challenge of managing tensions with the United States and seeking a solution to the problem of its nuclear proliferation.

North Korea has tried to maintain good relations with **China**. Still, it has also faced the challenge of managing tensions with this country.

South Korea has adopted a strategy of economic openness and international integration to promote its economic growth and strengthen its international position. It also sought to manage tensions with North Korea and promote regional peace and stability. It has developed a strong alliance with the United States and sought to maintain good relations with China and other regional countries.

ON THE OTHER HAND, SOUTH KOREA HAS ADOPTED WESTERN ECONOMIC AND POLITICAL MODELS AND SOUGHT TO ESTABLISH POSITIVE RELATIONS WITH ITS NEIGHBOURS AND THE UNITED STATES. However, it also faced the challenge of managing tensions with North Korea and seeking a solution to the problem of nuclear proliferation.

TAIWAN, HONG KONG AND MACAO have all had complex relations with China and have faced the challenge of managing tensions with China and maintaining their autonomy.

They faced the challenge of maintaining political and

economic autonomy as they sought to manage tensions with China and maintain good relations with their international trading partners.

Taiwan faced the challenge of managing tensions with China, considering the island part of its territory and trying to maintain its independence and sovereignty. It has also sought to develop relations with other countries through trade and cultural agreements.

THE GEOPOLITICAL SITUATION OF THE COUNTRIES OF SOUTHEAST ASIA

Southeast Asia is a geographical region that includes many countries in the southern part of East Asia. Some of the countries in Southeast Asia are:

1.	Viet Nam	7.	Brunei
2.	Laos	8.	Singapore
3.	Cambodia	9.	Indonesia
4.	Myanmar	10.	Filipino
5.	Thailand	11.	East Timor
6.	Malaysia		

This list may not be exhaustive, as the definition of "Southeast Asia" may vary depending on the context.

The geopolitical situation of Southeast Asia is complex and constantly changing, as each country has unique challenges and opportunities and plays an important role in the region differently.

SOME OF THE GEOPOLITICAL ISSUES THAT HAVE IMPACTED
THE REGION IN RECENT YEARS COULD BE SUMMARIZED:

Territorial tensions: Many countries in Southeast Asia
have faced territorial disputes, particularly over islands and
territorial waters in the South China Ocean.

Climate change: Many countries in Southeast Asia are
particularly vulnerable to the effects of climate change, such
as hurricanes, floods and droughts, and have faced the
challenge of managing these phenomena.

Terrorism: Some Southeast Asian countries have faced
the problem of terrorism and had to work to prevent attacks
and protect their citizens.

Transition to a market economy: Many countries in
Southeast Asia have faced the challenge of moving from
planned to market economies and adopting Western
economic and political models.

Ethnic minorities: Some countries in Southeast Asia
faced the challenge of managing tensions between different
ethnic minorities and promoting equality and tolerance.

Relations with China: Many Southeast Asian countries
have had complex relations with China, an important
regional geopolitical force.

JAPAN

JAPANESE GEOPOLITICS, INTERNATIONAL POLITICS AND INTERNATIONAL POLITICAL STRATEGY IN THE LAST TWENTY YEARS

Over the past two decades, several challenges and opportunities have influenced Japan's geopolitics, international politics, and political strategy.

Some of the geopolitical issues that have impacted Japan in recent years could be:

Relations with China: Japan has had a complex relationship with China, an important regional geopolitical force. It faced the challenge of managing tensions with China, particularly concerning territorial disputes and security issues.

North Korea Challenge: Japan has faced the challenge of North Korea's nuclear proliferation and has worked with the United States and other countries to seek a solution to the problem.

Managing tensions with the United States: Japan has had a close relationship with the United States, its main ally, but has also faced the challenge of managing tensions with this country.

Development of economic relations: Japan has developed its economic relations with foreign countries and faced the challenge of facing global competition and promoting innovation and economic growth.

Climate change: Japan has been affected by some of the effects of climate change, such as hurricanes, and has faced the challenge of managing these phenomena and promoting environmental sustainability.

Japan is an important geopolitical power globally and regionally. It has a strategic geographical position in the Pacific, with access to important sea and air trade routes. It is also one of the largest economies in the world and a major exporter of goods and services.

Japan has a history of security and stability and has played an important role in promoting regional peace and stability through its role as an ally of the United States in the region.

It also has a history of **economic and political cooperation with regional countries, such as China and ASEAN countries.** In addition, it has worked to promote trade and cultural exchanges.

Japan has been an important player in the fight against climate change and in promoting environmental sustainability worldwide. He has also *played a leadership role in promoting technology and innovation*.

In summary, Japan's geopolitical importance lies in its strategic geographical location, strong economy, and role in promoting peace and stability in the region.

SUMMARY IN CHRONOLOGICAL ORDER OF THE MILESTONES OF THE LAST TWENTY YEARS OF INTERNATIONAL POLITICS AND POLITICAL STRATEGY OF JAPAN

1.   2003: Japan participates in the international coalition's peacekeeping mission in Iraq, sending logistical support troops. This decision was controversial due to the Japanese Constitution's limitations on using military force.

2.   2010: Japan hosts the Winter Olympic Games in Vancouver.

3.   2011: Japan is hit by a magnitude 9.0 earthquake, tsunami, and nuclear catastrophe. The government's response to the crisis has been criticized by many for its slowness and lack of protective measures.

4.   2012: The Democratic Party of Japan, led by Shinzo Abe, wins the general election, and Abe becomes Prime Minister.

5.   2013: Japan revises its defence policy, expanding the role of its military force, known as the Self-Defense Forces (SDF).

6.   2015: Japan adopts a new defence law allowing the SDF to intervene in international conflicts to protect national interests and citizens.

7.   2017: Japan reached a trade agreement with the United States, known as the Trans-Pacific Partnership Treaty (TPP).

8.   2018: Japan hosts the Tokyo Summer Olympic Games.

9.   2019: Shinzo Abe resigns as Prime Minister for health reasons and is replaced by Yoshihide Suga.

10.   2020: Japan is affected by the COVID-19 pandemic, which has significantly impacted the country's economy.

WESTERN ASIA

GEOPOLITICS OF WEST ASIAN COUNTRIES

West Asia is a geographical and cultural region located between Europe and Asia that includes the following countries:

1. Armenia

2. Azerbaijan

3. Georgia

4. Iran

5. Iraq

6. Israel

7. Jordan

8. Kuwait

9. Lebanon

10. Oman

11. Qatar

12. Saudi Arabia

13. Syria

14. Turkey

15. United Arab Emirates

16. Yemen

West Asia has long been a strategic transit area for trade and travel. It is still a region of great geopolitical importance today. The countries of West Asia all have rich and diverse histories and cultures. They are characterized by various landscapes, ranging from mountains to plains.

The geopolitics of West Asian countries is influenced by many factors, such as their geographical location, natural resources, relations with their neighbours and world powers, and their internal political histories.

The **geopolitics of West Asian countries** is complex and constantly changing; therefore, it is difficult to summarize the elements and geopolitical situation relevant to each country over the last twenty years in a synthetic way.

However, there are some general trends and challenges that have affected the geopolitics of the region over the past twenty years:

Internal conflicts: Many West Asian countries, such as Iraq, Afghanistan and Syria, have faced many internal conflicts and have lived under the rule of authoritarian regimes over the past two decades. These conflicts have had a significant impact on the geopolitics of the region.

Resource producers: Some West Asian countries, such as **Iran, Iraq and Azerbaijan,** are major oil producers and other natural resources. The production and trade of these resources have played an important role in the region's geopolitics over the past twenty years.

International relations: Many West Asian countries have close relations with European Union countries and are members of the UN. International relations have influenced the region's geopolitics over the past twenty years.

Cultural and religious influences: Many West Asian countries are at the crossroads of different cultures and religions, which can affect their geopolitics. For example, the Israeli-Palestinian conflict is an issue of great geopolitical importance in the region.

These are just a few examples of the trends and challenges that have affected the geopolitics of West Asian countries over the past two decades.

West Asia is a vast and diverse region with many countries with complex geopolitical situations.

Here is a brief summary of the elements and geopolitical situation of some of the countries of Western Asia over the past twenty years:

Afghanistan: The last twenty years have been marked by civil war and the presence of foreign troops, both from NATO and other nations. Afghanistan is also an important transportation corridor for Central Asian gas and oil.

Armenia: Armenia has had difficulty establishing stable relations with its neighbours, especially with Azerbaijan, due to the Nagorno-Karabakh conflict. In addition, Armenia is also linked to Russia, both militarily and economically.

Azerbaijan: Azerbaijan is a major oil and gas producer and has established trade relations with many Western countries. However, it also had conflicts with Armenia because of Nagorno-Karabakh and Iran because of the division of Caspian Sea resources.

Bahrain: Bahrain is a small island state with a strong US military presence. It has had tensions with Iran because of its relationship with the United States and its position as a regional trading hub.

Georgia: Georgia has tried to establish closer relations with the West but has had difficulty managing its relations with Russia because of separatist conflicts in Abkhazia and South Ossetia and economic sanctions imposed by Russia.

Iran: Iran has been at the centre of numerous geopolitical tensions over the past two decades, mainly because of its nuclear program and sanctions imposed by the United States and the European Union. However, it has also played an essential role in the region as a religious and military power.

Iraq: Iraq has been the scene of numerous conflicts over the past two decades, mainly due to the 2003 U.S. invasion and subsequent civil war. Iraq is also a major oil producer and has struggled to manage internal and regional rivalries about energy resources.

Jordan: Jordan is a stable country in an unstable region and has had positive relations with many Western countries. However, it has also faced the challenge of managing the arrival of many refugees from neighbouring countries, particularly Syria.

Kuwait: Kuwait is a small oil-rich state and has had close trade and political relations with many Western countries. However, it also faced the threat of ISIS and tension with Iran.

Lebanon: Lebanon is a Christian-majority country that has struggled to maintain internal stability due to religious and political divisions. In addition, it has been influenced by conflicts in Syria and Israel.

Oman's robust oil-based economy has had positive relations with many Western countries. However, it has also faced tensions with neighbouring states, notably Yemen.

Qatar: Qatar is a small state rich in natural gas that has had close trade and political relations with many Western countries. However, it has also been at the centre of a diplomatic crisis with some of its neighbours, particularly Saudi Arabia, the United Arab Emirates and Bahrain.

Syria: Syria has been the scene of a devastating civil war over the past two decades, killing hundreds of thousands and driving millions of refugees to flee abroad. Syria is also at the centre of numerous regional and international tensions.

Yemen: Yemen has been hit by civil war and a severe humanitarian crisis over the past two decades. In addition, it was the scene of a regional conflict between Saudi Arabia and Iran.

Turkey: Turkey is an important regional power and has sought to establish trade and political relations with many countries in Western Asia and the world. However, it has also had difficulty managing internal tensions, particularly with Kurdish minorities and the Islamic movement. In addition, he had tensions with Russia because of the conflicts in Syria. He had a complex relationship with the European Union and the United States.

United Arab Emirates: The United Arab Emirates is a federated state of seven emirates and a major oil producer. Over the past twenty years, they have sought to diversify the economy and established trade and political relations with many countries in Western Asia and the world. However, they also had tensions with Iran because of their relationship with the United States. They played an essential role in the military coalition that fought the Islamic State in Iraq and Syria.

INDIA

GEOPOLITICS, INTERNATIONAL POLITICS AND INDIA'S INTERNATIONAL POLITICAL STRATEGY OVER THE PAST TWENTY YEARS.

The most relevant aspects of India from a geopolitical perspective include the following:

1. **Its strategic geographical position**: INDIA STRADDLES THE SPICE ROUTE AND ITS BORDERS WITH PAKISTAN, CHINA, NEPAL, BHUTAN, BANGLADESH AND MYANMAR. This strategic position has made India the object of conquest and external influences for centuries.

2. **Its population**: India is the second most populated country in the world, with over 1.3 billion inhabitants. India's rapidly growing population and substantial domestic market make it an emerging economic powerhouse.

3. **Natural resources**: India is rich in natural resources, such as coal, oil, gas, iron, bauxite and uranium. These resources are vital to the country's economic development and its role as an emerging regional power.

4. **Relations with neighbouring countries**: India has complicated relations, especially with Pakistan and China. These relations have a significant impact on India's geopolitics and international strategy.

5. **Position as an emerging regional power**: In recent years, India has established itself as an emerging regional power in South Asia and has sought to increase its influence globally through trade, investment, and participation in international organizations.

India has sought to increase its influence globally over the past two decades through trade, investment and participation in international organizations:

Trade: India has signed numerous trade agreements with countries worldwide over the past twenty years, thus increasing its weight globally as an exporter and importer.

Investment: India has attracted a lot of foreign investment over the past two decades, becoming one of the most attractive destinations for international investors.

Participation in international organizations: India is a **member of** major international organizations such as the **UN, G20** and **OECD** and has sought to use these organizations to promote its interests and increase its influence globally.

Examples of how India has sought to promote peace and stability in the South Asian region through multilateralism and diplomacy over the past two decades include:

Participation in regional organizations: India is a **member of** major regional organizations such as **SAARC (Association of Southeast Asian Nations) and ASEAN (Association of Southeast Asian Nations**) and has sought to use these organizations to promote economic cooperation and stability in the region.

Dialogue and negotiations: India has initiated numerous talks and negotiations with countries in its neighbourhood, particularly Pakistan and China, seeking to resolve tensions and promote peace and stability in the region.

Peace initiatives: India has launched several peace initiatives over the past two decades, such as **ASEAN's "Action Plan for Peace, Stability and Progress",** which aims to promote economic cooperation and dialogue.

SUMMARY OF THE MILESTONES OF THE LAST TWENTY YEARS OF INTERNATIONAL POLITICS AND POLITICAL STRATEGY OF INDIA:

1. 2003 – India becomes a Organisation for Economic Co-operation and Development (OECD) member.

2. 2004 - India is a permanent host of the Group of Eight (G8).

3. 2008 – India is admitted as a member of the Organization for the Prohibition of Chemical Weapons (OPCW).

4. 2009 – India is admitted to the Group of Twenty (G20).

5. 2010 – India is admitted as a plenipotentiary member of the Organization for Security and Co-operation in Europe (OSCE).

6. 2014 – India is admitted as a member of the Organization of Petroleum Exvasing Countries (OPEC).

7. 2016 – India is admitted as a member of the Missile Technology Control Regime (MTCR).

8. 2017 - India is admitted as a member of the Australia Group.

9. 2018 - India is admitted as a member of the Wassenaar Arrangement.

10. 2019 – India is admitted as a member of the Organization for the Prohibition of Chemical Weapons (OPCW).

CHINA

CHINA'S GEOPOLITICS, INTERNATIONAL POLITICS, AND INTERNATIONAL POLITICAL STRATEGY OVER THE PAST TWO DECADES.

China is a significant world power with a unique geographical location and history.

Geographically, China is the largest country in Asia and the third largest in the world, with a wide range of soils, climates and natural resources. China also has a long history and unique culture dating back over 4000 years.

Geopolitically, China is a permanent **member of the UN Security Council** and one of the world's leading powers. **China is also the largest trading partner of the United States and the second largest trading partner of the European Union**. However, China has had some conflicts with its neighbours, particularly with the South China Sea's uninhabited islands and Tibet. In addition, China has been criticized for its treatment of human rights and its role in the spread of COVID-19.

China is going through a period of rapid economic growth and military renewal, raising concerns about its intention to become the world's leading power. However, China says it is a peaceful power and wants to work with other countries to address global challenges. China is also a member of several regional and international organizations, such as the **Shanghai Cooperation Organization (SCO)** and **the Southeast Asia Regional Cooperation Association (ASEAN).**

The past two decades have seen several important geopolitical developments in China. Here are some of the most relevant aspects:

1. **Economic growth and development**: China has become one of the world's leading economies over the past two decades, with an average annual growth rate of 10% from 2001 to 2010. China's economic growth has significantly impacted the global economy and attracted a lot of foreign investment.

2. **Military Renewal:** China has invested significantly in military renewal over the past two decades to become a global military power. This has raised concerns about the possible threat to regional and international security.

3. **Territorial conflicts**: China has had territorial disputes with its neighbours over the past two decades, particularly with the South China Sea's uninhabited islands and Tibet. These conflicts have raised concerns about regional stability and the risk of military conflicts.

4. **Human rights treatment**: China has been criticized for its treatment of human rights, particularly its repression of ethnic minorities such as the Uyghurs in Xinjiang and its treatment of political dissidents.

China has followed a foreign policy based on "peace, development and cooperation" for the past two decades. It has promoted international cooperation to address global challenges and sought to become a global power through diplomacy, development aid and foreign investment. CHINA HAS ALSO SOUGHT TO PROMOTE ITS VISION OF A MULTIPOLAR WORLD ORDER AND TO DEVELOP TRADE AND SECURITY RELATIONS WITH COUNTRIES WORLDWIDE.

China has also sought to resolve territorial conflicts through diplomacy and has promoted regional integration through organizations such as the Shanghai Cooperation Organization (SCO) and the Southeast Asia Regional Cooperation Association (ASEAN).

China has sought to promote a development model based on cooperation and "JOINT PLANNING" to address global challenges like *climate change and poverty*. China has also promoted initiatives such as the BELT AND ROAD INITIATIVE, **which aims to build infrastructure and promote economic cooperation in Asia, Europe and Africa.**

China has also adopted a more assertive foreign policy in some regions, such as the South China Sea and Tibet, and has had conflicts with its neighbours.

However, China has faced challenges in its foreign policy over the past two decades.

For example, it has been criticized for its treatment of human rights and its role in the spread of COVID-19, which has damaged its global image.

China has had territorial conflicts with its neighbours and has raised concerns about its military renewal and ambitions to become a global power.

US Overtaken by China as a Global Trade Power — Data Driven

China's international policy and strategy over the past two decades have been primarily driven by its economic growth and desire to become a global power.

CHINA HAS ADOPTED A POLICY OF "OPENING UP AND REFORM", ALLOWING ITS ECONOMY TO INCREASE THROUGH FOREIGN INVESTMENT AND INTERNATIONAL TRADE.

China has adopted a "respect for sovereignty and territorial integrity" policy. That has sought to protect its national interests and has had some territorial conflicts with its neighbours.

HERE IS A CHRONOLOGICAL SUMMARY OF THE MILESTONES OF THE LAST TWENTY YEARS OF CHINA'S INTERNATIONAL POLITICS AND POLITICAL STRATEGY:

1. 2001: China joins the World Trade Organization (WTO).

2. 2001-2010: China has an average annual growth rate of 10%.

3. 2009: Representatives of BRICS (Brazil, Russia, India, China and South Africa) meet for the first time in Yekaterinburg, Russia, to discuss opportunities for economic cooperation. China becomes a founding member of the BRICS.

4. 2010: China becomes the largest trading partner of the United States.

5. 2013: China launches the Belt and Road Initiative, a series of infrastructure projects in Asia, Europe and Africa.

6. 2013: China becomes the European Union's second-largest trading partner.

7. 2014: China begins building a series of artificial islands in the South China Sea, raising concerns about territorial conflicts with its neighbours, especially regional stability and fishing rights.

8. 2014: China begins implementing security measures in the Xinjiang region to counter-terrorism, raising human rights concerns.

9. 2015: China joins the Paris Climate Agreement, committing to reduce greenhouse gas emissions.

10. 2015: China adopts a new national security law that is criticized for cracking down on ethnic minorities and political dissidents.

11. 2015: China adopts a new "peace and development" policy that aims to work with other countries to address global challenges.

12. 2017: China is accused of cracking down on ethnic minorities, particularly Uighurs in Xinjiang, raising human rights concerns.

13. 2019: China signs the Pacific International Trade Agreement to promote trade and investment between Asia-Pacific countries.

14.   2020: China becomes the largest trading partner of the United States and the second-largest trading partner of the European Union

AUSTRALIA AND NEW ZEALAND

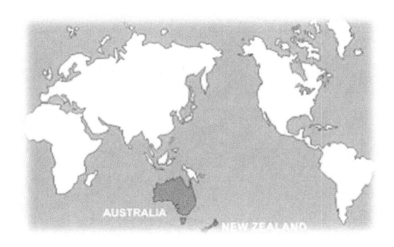

THE GEOPOLITICS, INTERNATIONAL POLITICS AND INTERNATIONAL POLITICAL STRATEGY OF AUSTRALIA AND NEW ZEALAND OVER THE PAST TWENTY YEARS

Australia and New Zealand's geopolitics were influenced by their geographical location in Oceania and their relations  with Asia and the Pacific countries. Over the past two decades, both countries have developed close trade and security relations with their Asia-Pacific neighbours, particularly China.

However, both have also maintained strong ties with the United States and the European Union, notably through the free trade agreement between Australia, New Zealand and the European Union.

In addition, both countries have developed strong cooperation on regional security issues, such as stability in East Timor and Papua New Guinea, and have participated in international peacekeeping missions.

Overall, the international policy of Australia and New Zealand over the past two decades has been characterised by a strong orientation towards international trade and cooperation. As well as a commitment to maintaining peace and stability in the region.

Australia

AUSTRALIA

There have been several significant geopolitical developments that have affected Australia over the past twenty years. Here are some of them:

China's growth: China has become one of Australia's top trading destinations in recent decades. Today, it is its largest trading partner. China's economic growth has also significantly impacted the Australian economy regarding trade opportunities and challenges.

Climate change: Australia is particularly vulnerable to the effects of climate change and has taken many measures to reduce its greenhouse gas emissions. It has also worked with other countries to promote global action on climate change.

Refugee crisis: In recent years, Australia has faced a refugee crisis, with increasing numbers of people trying to arrive in Australia by sea. This has raised difficult questions about immigration policies and human rights.

Relations with the United States: Australia has a **close historical relationship with the United States**, and the two countries have a defence agreement that provides for the presence of US troops in Australia. However, the report has *tension, particularly regarding regional security management and trade.*

Regional challenges: Australia also **faces regional challenges, such as stability in East Timor and Papua New Guinea** and the *risk of territorial conflicts in some areas of its maritime space.*

New Zealand

There have been several significant geopolitical developments that have NEW ZEALAND affected New Zealand over the past twenty years. Here are some of them:

China's growth: In recent decades, China has become one of New Zealand's main trading partners, and today it is its largest trading partner.

China's economic growth has also significantly impacted the New Zealand economy in terms of business opportunities and challenges.

Climate change: New Zealand is particularly vulnerable to the effects of climate change, mainly due to its geographical location and agriculture-based economy. It has taken several measures to reduce its greenhouse gas emissions. In addition, it has worked with other countries to promote global action on climate change.

Banking sector reforms: In recent years, New Zealand has undertaken a series of banking and financial sector reforms to increase the stability and transparency of the system.

These reforms have had a significant impact on the country's economy and have helped to strengthen its financial position.

Relations with Australia: New Zealand has a close relationship with Australia, with the two countries having a free trade agreement and cooperating on regional security issues.

However, the relationship has tension, particularly in trade and security management.

Regional challenges: New Zealand also faces regional challenges, such as stability in East Timor and Papua New Guinea and the risk of territorial conflicts in some areas of its maritime space.

SUMMARY OF THE MILESTONES OF THE LAST TWENTY YEARS OF INTERNATIONAL POLITICS AND POLITICAL STRATEGY OF AUSTRALIA AND NEW ZEALAND

Here are some milestones in international politics and the political strategy of Australia and New Zealand over the past two decades:

Free Trade Agreement between Australia, New Zealand and the European Union (2000): This agreement strengthened trade and political relations between the three countries and promoted trade in goods, services and investment.

Australian military intervention in Afghanistan (2001): Australia participated in the US-led international coalition in the war in Afghanistan, sending troops to fight terrorism and stabilize the country.

New Zealand military intervention in Iraq (2003): New Zealand participated in the US-led international coalition in the Iraq War, sending troops to help stabilize the country.

Both countries have participated in several international peacekeeping missions over the past two decades, including the intervention in East Timor and contributing to the UN missions in Afghanistan and Iraq.

Challenges to relations with China: Both countries have had moments of tension in their relationship with China over the past two decades, particularly concerning trade and regional security.

However, they have also developed close trade and cooperation relations with China.

Joining the Paris Agreement on climate change (2015): A global agreement that aims to reduce greenhouse gas emissions and combat climate change}.

A free trade agreement with the European Union: In 2020, Australia and New Zealand signed a free trade agreement with the European Union.

SOUTH AMERICA

GEOPOLITICS, INTERNATIONAL POLITICS AND THE INTERNATIONAL POLITICAL STRATEGY OF THE COUNTRIES OF SOUTH AMERICA 2000-2021

The geopolitics of South America over the past twenty years has been characterized by several significant changes and developments. One of the main factors that influenced **the international politics of South American countries was the increase in China's economic and political influence on the continent.** China has become an important trading partner for many South American countries, offering loans and investments in exchange for access to the continent's natural resources.

Over the past two decades, many countries in South America have experienced significant political changes, such as the collapse of military dictatorships in Brazil and Argentina and the rise of leftist governments in several nations, such as Venezuela and Bolivia.

These changes have had an impact on the international politics of the continent. In addition, they have affected relations with other countries of the world.

The **global economic crisis of 2008** had a significant impact on the economy of South America. In addition, it led to an increase in inequality and poverty in many countries on the continent. Over the past twenty years, this has increased political and social tension in many South American countries.

In general, the international political strategy of the countries of South America over the past twenty years has been characterized by greater regional cooperation and integration to promote economic growth and sustainable development.

Many South American countries have also sought to strengthen their relations with European Union and Latin American countries and to play a more active role in international organizations such as the Organization of American States (OAS) and the Union of South American Nations (UNASUR).

Brazil, Argentina, Chile and Colombia

The countries in South America considered most relevant from a geopolitical point of view are Brazil, Argentina, Chile and Colombia.

Brazil is the largest country in South America in terms of area and population. In addition, it has a geographical position of great importance due to its long Atlantic coast and its proximity to the Caribbean. Brazil is also one of the largest economies on the continent and has a leadership role in the region.

> **Brazil** is the largest country in South America in terms of area and population. It has a long Atlantic coastline and a strong presence in the Caribbean. Brazil is also one of the largest economies on the continent and has a leading position in the region. It has vital agriculture, manufacturing industry and services. It is a major coffee, sugar, oil and iron exporter. Brazil is a founding member of the Union of South American Nations (UNASUR) and the Community of Latin American and Caribbean States (CELAC).

Argentina is the second largest country in South America. It has a diversified economy with strong agriculture, manufacturing industry and services. Argentina also has a prominent geographical position, as it is located on the Atlantic coast and has a strong presence in the energy market.

Argentina is the second largest country in South America. It has a diversified economy with strong agriculture, manufacturing industry and services. It is also a major exporter of wheat, cocoa and wine products. Argentina has an important geographical position, as it is located on the Atlantic coast and has a strong presence in the energy market. It is a **member of the Organization of American States (OAS) and the Union of South American Nations (UNASUR)**

Chile is a country of great importance from a geopolitical point of view due to its geographical position along the coast of the Pacific Ocean and its stable economy based on the **export of mineral products such as copper.** Chile is also an important trading partner for many North American and Asia countries.

Chile is also an important trading partner for many North American and Asia countries. It is a member of the Organization for Economic Co-operation and Development (OECD) and the Union of South American Nations (UNASUR).

Colombia is another important country in South America from a geopolitical point of view. It is located on the Caribbean coast and has a strong **economy based on exporting products such as oil and coffee**. Colombia also has a prominent position in the region because of its relations with other Latin American countries.

Colombia is a member of the Organization of American States (OAS) and the Union of South American Nations (UNASUR).

Political relations between the countries of South America underwent significant changes from 2000 to 2021.

There were also many conflicts and tensions between the countries of South America during this period. One example is the *territorial conflict between Brazil and Guyana French, which intensified in 2015 when Brazil accused Guyana of illegally expanding its maritime borders*. In addition, there have been conflicts between countries in the region regarding economic issues, such as trade and investment.

Another significant development has been a political change in many South American countries. There have been many government changes during this period, including the election of new leaders and the adoption of new policies. For example, in many countries in the region, there has been an increase in populist movements and leaders promoting protectionist and nationalistic policies.

Political relations between South American countries remained complex and constantly evolving from 2000 to 2021. There have been efforts to promote regional cooperation and integration. Still, there have also been many conflicts and tensions between the region's countries.

BRICS AND SOUTH AMERICA

The BRICS are a group of five emerging countries, namely Brazil, Russia, India, China and South Africa, which have established a partnership to promote economic and political cooperation. The BRICS were established in 2010 and had increasing weight globally regarding the economy, population and military power.

South America is not a country that is part of the BRICS. Still, some South America countries, such as Brazil and Chile, have established partnership relations with the BRICS. For example, *Brazil and China have established a strategic partnership, which includes trade and investment between the two countries*.

Brazil has a trade history with China and has participated in several initiatives with the BRICS, such as the BRICS Monetary Fund.

Chile has also had trade relations with the **BRICS** and has participated in several initiatives. In addition, **Chile became the first South American country to sign a free trade agreement with China in 2005.**

In general, the BRICS and the countries of South America have growing economic and political relations. Still, they are not part of the same organization.

However, the BRICS and South American countries are interested in promoting global economic and political cooperation. Therefore, they could work together on issues of common interest.

SUMMARY OF THE MILESTONES OF THE LAST TWENTY YEARS OF INTERNATIONAL POLITICS AND POLITICAL STRATEGY OF THE COUNTRIES OF SOUTH AMERICA:

2000-2001: Establishment of the **Community of Latin American and Caribbean States (CELAC)** to promote economic and political cooperation between the countries of South America.

2002: **The Union of South American Nations (UNASUR)** is established as a regional integration organization.

2003: **MERCOSUR**, a regional integration organization comprising Argentina, Brazil, Paraguay and Uruguay, is expanded to include Venezuela.

2004: The election of Hugo Chávez as president of Venezuela, followed by a series of political and economic reforms that have impacted the region.

2005: Creation of the **Union of South American Nations (UNASUR)** to promote regional integration and cooperation among the countries of South America.

2005: Venezuela becomes a member of Mercosur, followed by Paraguay in 2012.

2006: Venezuela launches **PetroCaribe**, an energy cooperation program with Caribbean countries.

2006-2009: Election of Evo Morales as president of Bolivia, followed by a series of reforms that impacted the country's domestic politics and political strategy.

2008: Argentina and Brazil sign a military cooperation agreement, the first of its kind between the two countries.

2008: Election of Barack Obama as President of the United States, followed by a change in U.S. foreign policy toward South American countries.

2009: The election of Rafael Correa as president of Ecuador, followed by a series of reforms that have impacted the country's domestic politics and political strategy.

2009: **Brazil becomes a member of the G20,** an international economic and financial cooperation forum.

2010-2019: The election of Mauricio Macri as president of Argentina, followed by economic and political reforms that have impacted the region.

2010: The **Community of Latin American and Caribbean States (CELAC)** is a regional integration organization that includes all Latin American and Caribbean countries except the United States and Canada.

2013: **Chile hosts** the **APEC (Economic Cooperation for Asia-Pacific) summit,** an international forum for economic cooperation in Asia-Pacific.

2014: Election of Jair Bolsonaro as president of Brazil, followed by a series of changes in the country's domestic policy and political strategy.

2015: **Brazil hosts the COP 21 summit** and the United Nations summit on climate change.

2019: The election of Alberto Fernández as president of Argentina, followed by changes in the country's domestic politics and political strategy.

2019: **Brazil launches the Amazon Cooperation Forum,** an initiative to promote cooperation between the countries of the Amazon.

2020: **Argentina and Chile signed a military cooperation agreement**, the first of its kind between the two countries. It has significantly impacted South American countries' international politics and political strategy.

Canada

CANADA'S GEOPOLITICS, INTERNATIONAL POLITICS AND INTERNATIONAL POLITICAL STRATEGY OVER THE PAST TWENTY YEARS

Canada's geopolitics is influenced by its position in North America, alongside the United States, and its history as a British colony.

ALTHOUGH CANADA IS INDEPENDENT, IT STILL HAS A **STRONG RELATIONSHIP WITH THE UK**. IN ADDITION, IT PARTICIPATES IN MANY INTERNATIONAL ACTIVITIES THROUGH ITS INVOLVEMENT IN INTERNATIONAL ORGANISATIONS SUCH AS **THE COMMONWEALTH AND THE UNITED NATIONS ORGANISATION**.

Canada also maintains close ties with the United States, its leading trading partner and military ally.

Despite this close relationship, Canada has sought to maintain some autonomy and has adopted different positions than the United States on some important international issues.

Another vital aspect of Canada's geopolitics is its ethnic and cultural diversity. The country has a population composed of a wide range of ethnic and cultural groups and strives to maintain harmony between them.

Canada is also known for its immigration and refugee policy, allowing many people from different countries and cultures to settle there.

Canada's geopolitics is influenced by its geographical location, history, international relations and cultural diversity.

Over the past two decades, Canada's international politics and political strategy have focused on multilateral diplomacy and promoting democratic values and human rights.

Canada has actively participated in several international organizations, such as the United Nations and the G7. In addition, it has sought to promote peaceful solutions to international conflicts through dialogue and diplomacy.

Canada has also sought to promote international economic cooperation through adherence to trade treaties such as *the Canada-United States Free Trade Agreement (NAFTA) and the Paris Agreement on climate change.*

The country has also advocated for sustainable development. As a result, it has made significant progress in promoting the fight against climate change and adopting sustainable environmental practices.

In addition, Canada has sought to promote international security through its *participation in UN peacekeeping missions and collaboration with international allies, such as the United States*.

However, Canada has also sought to maintain some autonomy in its foreign policy and has often adopted different positions than the United States on important issues, such as trade and climate change.

SUMMARY OF THE MILESTONES OF THE LAST TWENTY YEARS OF INTERNATIONAL POLITICS AND CANADA'S POLITICAL STRATEGY

Below is a chronological, concise list of milestones from 2000 to 2021 in the international policy and political strategy of the countries of Canada:

2000-2010

1.   Participation in the United Nations peacekeeping mission in Afghanistan (2002)

2.   Joining the international coalition invading Iraq (2003)

3.   The signing of the Free Trade Agreement between Canada and the United States (NAFTA) (2004)

4.   G8 Presidency and commitment to combating climate change and sustainable development (2005)

5.   Participation in the United Nations peacekeeping mission in Haiti (2006)

6.   The signing of the Paris Agreement on climate change (2008)

7.   G20 Presidency and commitment to international economic cooperation (2009)

2010-2020

1.	Withdrawal from the United Nations peacekeeping mission in Afghanistan (2011)

2.	Adoption of a new National Security Strategy focusing on countering terrorism and violent extremism (2015)

3.	The signing of the Trans-Pacific Partnership for Economic Cooperation (TPP-11) (2016)

4.	G7 Presidency and commitment to gender equality and women's empowerment (2017)

5.	The signing of the Paris Agreement on legal migration (2018)

6.	Participation in the UN peacekeeping mission in Mali (2019)

2020-2021

1.	Participation in the UN peacekeeping mission in Lebanon (2020)

2.	The signing of the Paris Agreement on Food Security (2021)

CENTRAL AMERICA

GEOPOLITICS, INTERNATIONAL POLITICS AND THE INTERNATIONAL POLITICAL STRATEGY OF THE COUNTRIES OF CENTRAL AMERICA IN THE LAST TWENTY YEARS

The countries of Central America are: *Belize - Costa Rica - El Salvador - Guatemala - Honduras - Nicaragua - Panama*

Central America is a geographical region between North and South America and includes seven independent countries. The region is washed by the Caribbean Sea to the east and the Pacific Ocean to the west.

Central America is a region of great importance for international trade, as it includes the Panama Canal, one of the most important sea routes in the world.

The **geopolitics** of Central American countries is influenced by their geographical location between the United States and South America, as well as their natural resources and economy.

The United States is the region's leading trading partner and ally but also a source of concern for some countries because of its immigration and drug trafficking policies.

In addition, U.S. influence in the region has been debated due to its history of military interventions and support for authoritarian regimes.

Central America's geographical location makes it a transit region for drug trafficking from South America to the United States. This has led to a growing concern about security and the fight against drug trafficking.

THE ECONOMY OF CENTRAL AMERICAN COUNTRIES IS PRIMARILY BASED ON AGRICULTURE. STILL, SOME COUNTRIES ALSO HAVE SIGNIFICANT OIL, GAS AND MINERALS RESERVES.

However, dependence on natural resources has also created economic vulnerabilities due to commodity price volatility.

Urbanization and climate change are having an impact on the geopolitics of the region. In particular, increasing urbanization creates housing, transport and public services challenges.

Moreover, climate change is putting natural resources and coastal communities at risk.

The **international politics** of the Central American countries from 2000 to 2021 was influenced by several factors, such as relations with the United States, the European Union and other Latin American countries, security, the fight against drug trafficking and the stabilization of political regimes.

Many Central American countries have sought to strengthen their relations with the European Union and other Latin American countries through trade agreements and membership in international organizations such as **the Organization of American States (OAS) and the Rio Group**.

 In addition, many Central American countries have faced challenges regarding stabilising their political regimes, such as democratic elections and respect for human rights. As a result, many have sought to promote peace and stability through dialogue and diplomacy.

As for **international political strategy**, many Central American countries have sought to promote economic growth and sustainable development through increased foreign investment and international trade.

Summary of the fundamental stages of the last twenty years of international politics and political strategy of the countries of Central America.

Here is a chronological and concise list of the fundamental stages of international politics and political strategy of the Central American countries from 2000 to 2021:

1.   2000: **Costa Rica joins the Organization of American States (OAS)**

2. **Panama signs a trade agreement with the European Union**

3. 2001: **Belize joins OAS**

4. 2002: **El Salvador signs a free trade agreement with the United States**

5. 2003: **Nicaragua signs a trade agreement with the European Union**

6. **Guatemala joins the OAS**

7. 2004: **El Salvador becomes the first Central American country to sign a free trade agreement with the European Union**

8. 2005: **Honduras joins OAS**

9. 2006: **Costa Rica signs a free trade agreement with the European Union**

10. 2007: **Guatemala, Honduras and Nicaragua sign a free trade agreement with the United States**

1. 2008: **Costa Rica, El Salvador, Guatemala, Honduras and Nicaragua joined the Rio Group,** a regional organization for economic cooperation and trade

2. 2009: **El Salvador signs a free trade agreement with Japan**

3. 2010: **Nicaragua signs a free trade agreement with Japan**

4. 2011: **Costa Rica, El Salvador, Guatemala, Honduras and Nicaragua join the Pacific Alliance**, a regional organization for economic cooperation and trade

5. 2012: **Panama signs a free trade agreement with Japan**

6. 2013: **El Salvador signs a free trade agreement with South Korea**

7. 2014: **Nicaragua signs a free trade agreement with South Korea**

8. 2015: **Costa Rica, El Salvador, Guatemala, Honduras and Nicaragua sign a free trade agreement with Canada**

9. 2016: **Costa Rica, El Salvador, Guatemala, Honduras and Nicaragua sign a free trade agreement with Chile**

10. 2017: **Costa Rica, El Salvador, Guatemala, Honduras and Nicaragua sign a free trade agreement with Mexico**

11. 2018: **Costa Rica, El Salvador, Guatemala, Honduras and Nicaragua join the Community of Latin American and Caribbean States (CELAC)**

12. 2019: **Panama joins the Pacific Alliance**

13. 2020: **Costa Rica, El Salvador, Guatemala, Honduras and Nicaragua join the Organization for Economic Co-operation and Development (OECD)**

14. 2021: **Belize signs a free trade agreement with Canada.**

MESSICO

GEOPOLITICS, INTERNATIONAL POLITICS AND MEXICO'S INTERNATIONAL POLITICAL STRATEGY

Mexico's geopolitics is influenced by many factors, such as its geographical location, natural resources, international relations, and domestic issues.

Mexico is located in Latin America and is the largest country in Central America. It has two coasts, one on the Pacific Ocean and the other on the Atlantic Ocean. Mexico borders the United States to the north and Guatemala and Belize to the south.

MEXICO IS RICH IN NATURAL RESOURCES, SUCH AS OIL, NATURAL GAS, COPPER AND SILVER. Mexico's natural resources represent an important source of income for the country. Still, at the same time, they can also be a source of tension with other countries or with foreign companies interested in accessing these resources.

MEXICO HAS A LONG HISTORY OF COMPLEX RELATIONS WITH THE UNITED STATES, ITS LEADING TRADING PARTNER. As a result, relations between the two countries are *often influenced by immigration, economic and security issues.*

Within Mexico, several internal issues affect the country's geopolitics, such as widespread poverty, social inequalities, drug trafficking, and violence related to organized crime. All these issues have an impact on Mexico's political stability and security.

Over the past two decades, Mexico's international policy has been characterized by a solid commitment to multilateralism and the promotion of peace and stability internationally.

Mexico has been an active member of the United Nations and has played an essential role in several UN peacekeeping missions worldwide.

Mexico was a founding member of the Community of Latin American and Caribbean States (CELAC), a regional organization that aims to promote cooperation between Latin American and Caribbean countries.

Mexico has also developed important relations with other countries, such as China, the European Union and the G20 nations.

Over the past twenty years, Mexico has also sought to strengthen its international presence through **participation in** several international organizations, such as the Organization for **Economic Co-operation and Development (OECD) and the G20.**

Mexico has sought to promote its regional leadership in Latin America and the Caribbean in the past two decades through cooperation and diplomacy.

SUMMARY OF THE MILESTONES OF THE LAST TWENTY YEARS OF INTERNATIONAL POLITICS AND POLITICAL STRATEGY IN MEXICO

Here is a chronological list of milestones in Mexico's international politics and political strategy from 2000 to 2021:

2000-2006: Mexico is a member of the G20 and actively participates in G20 meetings. Mexico also promotes regional cooperation in Latin America and the Caribbean by creating the Community of Latin American and Caribbean States (CELAC).

1. 2000: Mexico becomes a Organization for Economic Co-operation and Development (OECD) member.

2. 2003: Mexico participates in the United Nations peacekeeping mission in Haiti.

3. 2005: Mexico is elected a non-permanent United Nations Security Council member.

2006-2012: Mexico hosts the Conference of the Parties to the United Nations Framework Convention on Climate Change (COP16) in Cancún. Mexico also supports the creation of the Union of the Americas (UNASUR). This regional organization aims to promote cooperation and integration among Latin American countries.

1. 2006: Mexico becomes a member of the G20.

2. 2007: Mexico signs a free trade agreement with the European Union.

3. 2008: Mexico becomes a member of the Community of Latin American and Caribbean States (CELAC).

4.	2009: Mexico takes over the presidency of the Rio Group, an international organization that brings Latin American and Caribbean countries together.

5.	2011: Mexico hosts the Conference of the Parties to the United Nations Convention on Climate Change (COP 16).

2012-2018: Mexico is a non-permanent member of the UN Security Council and actively participates in UN peacekeeping missions. Mexico also promotes economic cooperation with China by creating the Grupo de Los Treinta (G30), which aims to promote economic cooperation between Latin American countries and China.

2018-2021: Mexico is a member of the G20 and will host the G20 presidency in 2021. Mexico also promotes regional cooperation in Latin America and the Caribbean through participation in the Alianza del Pacífico. This regional economic organization promotes integration and collaboration between Latin American and Asia-Pacific countries.

2021-2023: Mexico promotes international cooperation through participation in several international organizations, such as the OECD and the G20. Mexico also supports adopting a multilateral approach to global issues and promotes peace and stability worldwide.

1.	2020: Mexico participates in the United Nations peacekeeping mission in Mali.

2.   2021: Mexico becomes a World Trade Organization (WTO) member.

AFRICA

GEOPOLITICS, INTERNATIONAL POLITICS AND AFRICA'S INTERNATIONAL POLITICAL STRATEGY

In geopolitics, Africa can be divided into regions or subcontinents. Here are some of the most common subdivisions:

North Africa: includes the countries of North Africa, such as Egypt, Libya, Morocco and Tunisia.

West Africa: includes West African countries, such as Ghana, Senegal and Niger.

Central Africa: includes Central African countries, such as Cameroon, Congo and Gabon.

East Africa: includes East African countries, such as Kenya, Uganda and Rwanda.

Southern Africa: includes southern African countries, such as South Africa, Botswana and Zimbabwe.

Horn of Africa: includes the countries of the Horn of Africa, such as Ethiopia, Somalia and Eritrea.

Of course, these subdivisions are only indicative and do not fully reflect Africa's complex geopolitical reality. There are many other ways to divide the continent according to criteria such as geographical features, cultures and local economies.

THE GEOPOLITICS OF AFRICAN COUNTRIES IS A VERY COMPLEX TOPIC AND CANNOT BE COVERED IN A few lines. However, I can provide you with some general information:

1.   **AFRICA IS A CONTINENT RICH IN NATURAL RESOURCES, SUCH AS OIL, GAS, DIAMOND, GOLD AND PLATINUM, WHICH ATTRACT THE INTEREST OF MANY FOREIGN COUNTRIES.**

2.   Many African countries were colonized and are *still influenced by their former colonial powers*.

3.   **Poverty and inequality** are common problems in many African countries, despite recent progress in economic growth.

4.   *Africa has significant cultural and linguistic diversity, with over 2000 languages spoken.*

5.   **Political instability and armed conflict** have been common problems in many African countries. However, there has been progress in stabilising some regions in recent years.

6.   *Africa's growing role globally is becoming increasingly important for international trade and foreign investment.*

7.   *Africa is also a continent with a growing young and rapidly growing population,* representing an opportunity and a challenge for the future.

In Africa, several countries are considered "emerging", showing significant economic growth in recent years. Some of the most important emerging countries in Africa are:

213

Ghana: Ghana is one of the most stable and democratic countries on the continent and has seen sustained economic growth in recent years, thanks to the **expansion of exports of products such as gold, oil and cocoa**.

Senegal: Senegal is a country with a diversified and fast-growing economy, with a GDP growth rate of 6% per year. **Exports of products such as fish and phosphate** are boosting the country's economic growth.

Rwanda: Rwanda is one of the fastest-growing countries in Africa, with a GDP growth rate of 7% per year. Growth has been driven by the expansion of the service sector, especially **tourism and infrastructure development.**

Ethiopia: Ethiopia is one of the fastest-growing countries in Africa, with a GDP growth rate of 8% per year. Growth was driven by **infrastructure development and the expansion of the manufacturing sector.**

Mozambique: Mozambique has seen significant economic growth in recent years, thanks to the expansion of **exports of products such as coal and natural gas.**

Kenya: Kenya is one of the most critical emerging African countries and has seen sustained economic growth in recent years, thanks to the **expansion of the service sector, especially tourism and transport**.

No African country is universally recognized as a leader by all the other countries on the continent.

However, some countries have a leadership role in certain areas or sectors. For example:

Egypt: Egypt is the most populous country in North Africa and has a regional leadership role in the area, both politically and economically.

South Africa: South Africa is the largest country in southern Africa and has an economic and political leadership role.

Nigeria: Nigeria is the most populous country on the continent and has an economic leadership role in Africa, thanks to its large economy and its position as the continent's leading oil producer.

Ghana: Ghana is one of the most stable and democratic countries on the continent and has a political leadership role in West Africa.

Kenya: Kenya is an emerging country in East Africa and has a leadership role in the region, both politically and economically.

Ethiopia: Ethiopia is the most populous country in East Africa and has a political and military leadership role in the region.

GDP per capita of African countries 2020

Country	GDP	Country	GDP	Country	GDP	Country	GDP
Seychelles	12,323	Côte d'Ivoire	2,281	Ethiopia	974	Sierra Leone	518
Mauritius	8,951	Ghana	2,108	Lesotho	924	Madagascar	515
Gabon	7,185	Nigeria	2,149	Zimbabwe	922	CAF	480
GNQ	7,331	Congo, Rep	2,128	Uganda	915	Congo, DR	457
Botswana	6,558	Kenya	2,075	Mali	899	Mozambique	455
South Africa	4,736	Angola	2,021	Rwanda	823	Malawi	393
Namibia	4,002	STP	1,912	Burkina Faso	769	South Sudan	303
Egypt	3,561	Mauritania	1,791	Guinea-Bissau	767	Burundi	264
Eswatini	3,415	Cameroon	1,493	Gambia	746	Somalia	225
Cape Verde	3,358	Senegal	1,455	Sudan	735		
Algeria	3,331	Comoros	1,337	Togo	690		
Tunisia	3,295	Benin	1,259	Liberia	654		
Libya	3,282	Tanzania	1,105	Chad	640		
Morocco	3,121	Guinea	1,019	Eritrea	585		
Djibouti	3,074	Zambia	1,001	Niger	536		

THE MOST RELEVANT GEOPOLITICAL ELEMENTS OF AFRICAN COUNTRIES DEPEND ON THE COUNTRY IN QUESTION AND MAY INCLUDE THE FOLLOWING:

1. **Natural resources**: Many African countries are rich in natural resources, such as oil, gas, diamond, gold and platinum, which can have a significant impact on the country's geopolitics.

2. **Geographical location**: A country's geographical location can affect its geopolitics, for example, if it is located in a strategic region or near essential trade routes.

3. **Relations with neighbouring countries**: Relations with neighbouring countries can be an essential factor in the geopolitics of an African country, both in terms of trade and security.

4. **Political** stability: Political instability and armed conflict have been common problems in many African countries and can significantly impact the country's geopolitics.

5. **Foreign powers**: Many African countries were colonized and are still influenced by their former colonial powers or other foreign powers.

6. **Economic development:** A country's level of economic growth can impact its geopolitics by attracting foreign investment or influencing relations with other countries.

Some of the African countries that play an essential role in the world economy are:

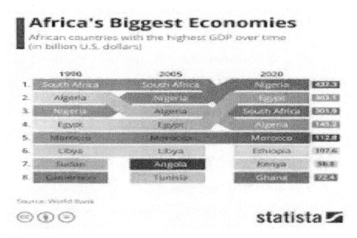

Africa's Biggest Economies

African countries with the highest GDP over time (in billion U.S. dollars)

	1980	2005	2020	
1.	South Africa	South Africa	Nigeria	432.3
2.	Algeria	Nigeria	Egypt	303.1
3.	Nigeria	Algeria	South Africa	301.9
4.	Egypt	Egypt	Algeria	145.2
5.	Morocco	Morocco	Morocco	112.8
6.	Libya	Libya	Ethiopia	107.6
7.	Sudan	Angola	Kenya	98.8
8.	Cameroon	Tunisia	Ghana	72.4

Source: World Bank

statista ◤

Nigeria: Nigeria is the continent's leading oil producer and one of the largest oil exporters in the world. Nigeria is also the most populous country on the continent and has one of Africa's largest economies.

Angola: Angola is one of Africa's *largest oil producers and a significant oil exporter worldwide*. Angola is also Africa's *second-largest diamond producer.*

South Africa: South Africa is Africa's *largest platinum producer and second largest gold producer*. South Africa is also a *major coal exporter* and has one of Africa's largest economies.

Egypt: Egypt is a significant *producer of natural gas and one of the world's largest gas exporters*. Egypt is also Africa's leading cotton producer and has one of the largest economies on the continent.

Ghana: Ghana is a significant *producer of gold and cocoa* and has one of the fastest-growing economies in Africa.

Morocco: Morocco is *a major phosphate producer and one of the world's largest phosphate exporters*. Morocco is also a *major producer of olive oil and cotton.*

SOME OF THE FOREIGN COUNTRIES THAT MADE SIGNIFICANT INVESTMENTS IN AFRICA BETWEEN 2000 AND 2021: CHINA, INDIA, THE UNITED STATES AND THE EUROPEAN UNION

China: China has invested much in Africa during this period, especially in the infrastructure sector. For example, *in many African countries, China has financed the construction of roads, bridges and railways*. Here are some examples of **China's investments in Africa:**

> **Infrastructure**: *China has financed many infrastructure projects in Africa, such as roads, bridges and railways.* For example, China funded the construction of the Addis Ababa-Djibouti railway, one of Africa's most significant infrastructure works.

> **Energy**: *China has invested in energy projects in Africa, such as constructing coal, gas and hydroelectric power plants*.

1. In 2013, China financed the construction of a 300 MW coal-fired power plant in Zambia.

2. In 2010, China financed the construction of a 250 MW hydroelectric power plant in Ghana.

3. In 2009, China financed the construction of a 300 MW coal-fired power plant in Zimbabwe.

Manufacturing: *China has made significant investments in manufacturing sectors in Africa, such as clothing, textiles and electronics.*

Agriculture: China has invested in agricultural projects in Africa, for example, through the creation of plantations or the purchase of agricultural land.

Services: China has invested in service sectors in Africa, such as tourism and trade.

Natural resources: China has invested in natural resource extraction projects in Africa, such as oil, gas and minerals.

1. In 2012, China bought natural resource mining company Anvil Mining, becoming one of the leading copper producers in Congo.

INDIA: India has also invested much in Africa during this period, especially in manufacturing and services.

Manufacturing: INDIA has made significant investments in manufacturing sectors in Africa, such as clothing, textiles and electronics.

Energy: INDIA has made many investments in energy projects in Africa, such as constructing coal and gas power plants.

1. In 2011, the Indian company Reliance Industries signed an agreement with the government of Mozambique to construct a 400 MW gas-fired power plant.

2. In 2016, the Indian company Adani Group signed an agreement to construct a 1,600 MW coal-fired power plant in Togo.

Agriculture: INDIA has invested in agricultural projects in Africa, for example, through the creation of plantations or the purchase of agricultural land.

Services: INDIA has invested in service sectors in Africa, such as tourism and trade.

1. In 2015, Indian company Tata Consultancy Services opened a business training centre in Ghana to provide consulting and training services in areas such as e-commerce and digital marketing.

2.   In 2012, Indian company Bharti Airtel bought a mobile phone company, Zain Africa, becoming the fourth largest mobile operator on the continent.

Natural resources: INDIA has invested in natural resource extraction projects in Africa, such as oil and gas.

1.   In 2009, the Indian company Essar Group bought the oil refining company Stanbic Bank, becoming one of the leading oil refiners in Africa.

Infrastructure: INDIA has financed some infrastructure projects in Africa, such as roads and bridges.

United States: The United States made significant investments in several African sectors and areas from 2000 to 2021. Here are some of the regions in which the United States has made significant investments in Africa during this period:

Energy: The United States has made many investments in energy projects in Africa, such as the construction of coal, gas and hydroelectric power plants.

1.   In 2019, the US company General Electric announced a $4 billion investment in energy projects in Egypt.

2.   In 2017, US company General Electric announced a $15 billion investment in energy projects in Africa by 2030.

3.   In 2016, the US company General Electric announced a $1 billion investment in energy projects in Egypt.

Agriculture: The United States has invested in agricultural projects in Africa, for example, through the creation of plantations or the purchase of agricultural land.

Services: The United States has invested in service sectors in Africa, such as tourism and trade.

1.   In 2018, the US company Marriott International announced the opening of nine new hotels in Africa, with an investment of about 500 million dollars.

2.   In 2018, the US company Blackstone Group announced an investment of 500 million dollars in real estate projects in Africa.

Natural resources: The United States has invested in natural resource extraction projects in Africa, such as oil, gas and minerals.

1.   In 2014, the US company GE Oil & Gas announced a $500 million investment in energy projects in Angola.

Infrastructure and Technology: The United States has financed the construction of some infrastructure projects in Africa, such as roads and bridges.

2.   In 2020, the US company Google announced an investment of 100 million dollars in broadband development projects in Africa.

3.   In 2017, the US company IBM announced a $100 million investment in a training centre for companies in Ghana.

4.   In 2016, the US firm Goldman Sachs announced an investment of 1 billion dollars in development projects in Africa.

1.   In 2015, the US company Procter & Gamble announced an investment of 1.4 billion dollars in development projects in Africa by 2020.

Russia made a lot of investments in Africa in different sectors and countries from 2000 to 2021. Here are some of the areas in which Russia has made significant investments in Africa during this period:

Energy: Russia has made many investments in energy projects in Africa, such as constructing coal and gas power plants.

1.   In 2014, the Russian company Gazprom signed an agreement to construct a 1,400 MW gas-fired power plant in Egypt.

2.   In 2013, the Russian company Rosatom signed an agreement to construct two nuclear power plants in Egypt.

Natural resources: Russia has invested in natural resource extraction projects in Africa, such as oil and gas.

1.   In 2017, the Russian company Rosneft signed an agreement to buy a 20% stake in the oil extraction company Glencore in Congo.

2.   In 2015, the Russian company Alrosa signed an agreement to buy a 25% stake in the diamond mining company Endiama in Angola.

Armaments: Russia has sold arms and military equipment to many African countries, becoming one of the continent's leading arms suppliers.

1.   In 2017, Russia signed an agreement to supply SU-35 combat aircraft to Egypt.

2.   In 2016, Russia signed an agreement to supply Mi-35 combat helicopters and air defence systems to Angola.

3.   In 2015, Russia signed an agreement to supply S-300 air defence systems to Egypt.

4.   In 2014, Russia signed an agreement to supply S-300 air defence systems to Algeria.

5.   In 2013, Russia signed an agreement to supply An-124 military transport aircraft to Angola.

Infrastructure: Russia has financed the construction of some infrastructure projects in Africa, such as roads and bridges.

1.   In 2016, the Russian company Rostec announced an investment of 1 billion dollars in development projects in Egypt.

Agriculture: Russia has invested in agricultural projects in Africa, for example, through the creation of plantations or the purchase of agricultural land.

Investment by **European Union countries** in Africa has increased significantly in recent years. Here are some examples of investments made by European Union countries in Africa from 2000 to 2021:

2.   In 2018, French Total announced a $1 billion investment in oil extraction projects in Egypt.

3.   In 2018, Spanish company Iberdrola announced a $3 billion investment in energy projects in Africa.

4.   In 2017, the German company Siemens announced a $1 billion investment in energy projects in Egypt.

5.   In 2017, French Total signed an agreement to buy a 10% stake in the oil extraction company ENI in Mozambique.

6.   In 2016, the French company Orange announced a $1 billion investment in telecommunications projects in Africa.

1.   In 2016, the German company Siemens announced an investment of 15 billion dollars in development projects in Africa by 2025.

2.   In 2015, the Italian company Eni announced a $1 billion investment in oil extraction projects in Egypt.

3.   In 2015, the Belgian company Heineken announced an investment of 200 million dollars in development projects in Africa by 2020.

4.   In 2014, the French company EDF announced a $1 billion investment in energy projects in Africa.

Internal Geopolitics

Several internal alliances in Africa have a significant geopolitical impact. Here are some of the most relevant internal alliances in Africa:

African Union (AU): The African Union is an intergovernmental organization that brings together all African countries. Its main objective is to promote the region's peace, stability and economic development.

Economic Community of West African Countries (ECOWAS): ECOWAS is a regional economic organization that brings together the countries of West Africa. Its objective is to promote trade and economic development in the region.

Southern African Development Community (SADC): The SADC is a regional organization that brings together the countries of Southern Africa. It aims to promote peace, stability and economic development in the region.

Common Market of Eastern and Southern Africa (COMESA): COMESA is a regional economic organization that brings together the countries of Eastern and Southern Africa. It aims to promote trade and economic development in the region.

This list is not exhaustive, and there have been many other significant developments in African countries' international politics and political strategy over the past twenty years.

SWITZERLAND

GEOPOLITICS AND INTERNATIONAL POLITICS AND SWITZERLAND'S INTERNATIONAL POLITICAL STRATEGY OVER THE LAST TWENTY YEARS

Switzerland is a small country with a crucial geographical position in the centre of Europe. Its political neutrality, which dates back to the end of the Thirty Years' War in the seventeenth century, has helped it become an important centre of international trade and mediation. Switzerland is known for its political stability and solid and diversified economy, making it one of the wealthiest countries in the world. Despite its neutrality, Switzerland is a member of some international organisations, such as the UN and the European Union. However, it is not a full member. Switzerland has very close relations with European countries and maintains good relations with the rest of the world.

Switzerland is an important international financial centre and plays a leading role in global financial regulation.

Over the past twenty years, Switzerland's international policy has been based primarily on political neutrality and the defence of democracy and human rights. Switzerland is active in many areas of international diplomacy and plays an essential role as a mediator in international conflicts. Switzerland is involved in various international organisations, such as the UN, the European Union and the Council of Europe, and participates in various peacekeeping missions worldwide.

Switzerland has also developed a robust economic security strategy based on diversifying exports and promoting trade with developing countries. In addition, Switzerland is an important international financial centre and plays a vital role in global financial regulation.

Over the past twenty years, Switzerland's international policy has been characterised by a solid commitment to global peace, security and development, and the defence of human rights and democracy.

WHAT INTERNATIONAL GEOPOLITICAL SIGNIFICANCE DOES SWITZERLAND HAVE

Switzerland is a small country, but it has significant international geopolitical significance due to its geographical position in the centre of Europe. Its substantial and diversified economy and its history of political neutrality. As a result, **Switzerland is an important centre of international trade and mediation**. It is **essential in various international organisations, such as the UN, the European Union and the Council of Europe**.

Switzerland is an important international financial centre and plays a leading role in global financial regulation. Switzerland is also known for its political stability, the tradition of democracy, and respect for human rights. This makes it a reliable partner for other countries in international relations.

Here is a list of milestones in Switzerland's international policy and political strategy from 2000 to 2021:

1. 2000: Switzerland joins the Schengen Agreement, which eliminates controls at the EU's internal borders.

2. 2003: Switzerland joins the **European Union as an associate member.**

3. 2004: Switzerland becomes a member of the **European Research Union.**

4. 2006: Switzerland votes to join the **European Energy Union.**

5. 2008: Switzerland signs a free trade agreement with **China**.

6. 2009: Switzerland votes to join the **European Union for tourism.**

7. 2011: Switzerland signs a **free trade agreement with the United States.**

8. 2014: Switzerland votes to join the European Union for the environment.

9. 2015: Switzerland adopts a new internal security policy, which creates a rapid reaction force to deal with possible threats to national security.

10. 2017: Switzerland votes to join the European Union for Culture.

11. 2019: Switzerland signs a **free trade agreement with Canada.**

12. 2020: Switzerland participates in negotiations for accession to the European Security Union.

13. 2021: Switzerland adopts a new economic security strategy based on diversifying exports and promoting trade with developing countries.

This list is not exhaustive, and there have been many other significant developments in Switzerland's international politics and political strategy over the past twenty years.

We can give a general overview of Caribbean countries' geopolitics and international politics over the past twenty years. Still, to get a more accurate and up-to-date picture, it may be necessary to do more in-depth research. So we will make a brief and concise overview with some in-depth analysis to allow you to continue now on your own. I believe this method has given you more knowledge of the geopolitical research and analysis method.

CARIBBEAN

GEOPOLITICS AND INTERNATIONAL POLITICS AND INTERNATIONAL POLITICAL STRATEGY OF CARIBBEAN COUNTRIES IN THE LAST TWENTY YEARS

Caribbean countries are a geographical region that includes a series of islands and countries located in the Atlantic Ocean, northeast of Latin America and southeast of the United States. Some of the best-known Caribbean countries are:

1. *Antigua and Barbuda*
2. *Bahamas*
3. *Barbados*
4. *Cuba*
5. *Dominica*
6. *Dominican Republic*
7. *Grenada*
8. *Jamaica*

9.	Haiti	13.	Saint Lucia
10.	Martinique	14.	Saint Vincent and the Grenadines
11.	Montserrat		
12.	Saint Kitts and Nevis	15.	Trinidad and Tobago

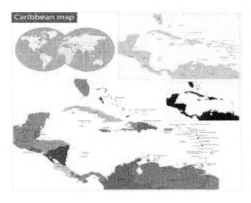

These countries share a common colonial history and an Afro-Caribbean culture. Still, they also have many unique cultural and linguistic elements. European powers, such as Spain, France and the United Kingdom colonised many of these countries. They gained independence in the 60s and 70s of the last century. However, due to their small size and dependence on the world economy, many of these countries still find it challenging to make their voices heard internationally.

Today, the Caribbean countries are heterogeneous economic and political regions, with some enjoying relative prosperity and stability and others suffering from poverty and political instability. An essential theme in the geopolitics of Caribbean countries is their relationship with the United States. The United States has a history of interference in the domestic politics of many of these countries. Also, it has a robust military presence in the region, with naval and air bases in many Caribbean countries. However, the United States is also an important trading partner for many Caribbean countries and has developed cooperative relations with many of these countries in the military, economic and political fields.

Another critical issue is the relationship between Caribbean countries with the rest of Latin America. *Many of these countries have developed cooperative relations with their Latin American neighbours.* They have participated in regional organizations such as the *Community of Spanish-speaking Countries (CPLS) and the Caribbean Community (CARICOM)*.

However, *the Caribbean region is also divided by historical rivalries and cultural and political differences, which can create tensions in relations between different countries*.

The international political strategy of Caribbean countries is often influenced by their economic priorities. Many of these countries heavily depend on tourism and agricultural and mineral product exports, making them vulnerable to global market fluctuations. As a result, many Caribbean countries have sought to diversify their economies and develop trade relationships with partners worldwide.

Over the past twenty years, Caribbean countries have faced several global geopolitical and political problems. One of the main themes was their relationship with the United States. Many of these countries have developed trade and military relations with the United States. Still, some have also expressed concerns about excessive U.S. influence in the region.

Another important theme was the relationship of Caribbean countries with the rest of Latin America. Many of these countries have developed cooperative relations with their Latin American neighbours.

Many Caribbean countries have sought to diversify their economies and develop trade relations with partners worldwide: to reduce their dependence on tourism, agricultural products, and mineral exports. However, some Caribbean countries have also faced domestic challenges like poverty, inequality, and ethnic and political tensions. In general, Caribbean countries' geopolitics and international politics over the past twenty years have been influenced by their small size, dependence on the world economy and their relations with the United States and other Latin American countries. Consequently, the international political strategy of these countries has been guided by their economic priorities and the goal of establishing themselves as independent actors on the international stage.

Cuba

Cuba is located in the Caribbean, about 150 km southwest of Key West, Florida.

It is the largest island in the Caribbean and the northernmost in the Antilles. It has a population of about 11 million and an area of 109,884 km².

Its geographical position in the Caribbean makes it a country of great strategic importance. Throughout history, it has been colonized by several European countries, including Spain, England and France. It has served as a base for pirates and corsairs. The United States has played a dominant role in the Caribbean region in recent centuries.

Cuba has been the subject of numerous international tensions and crises, particularly during the Cold War.

Today, Cuba is a country that has maintained complex relations with many countries in the region and the world. For example, it has had historically **close ties with Russia and other communist countries. Still, it has also sought to strengthen its relations with Latin American countries and the European Union.** In addition, it has **a robust military presence abroad, particularly in Africa, and has also participated in UN peacekeeping missions in other countrie**s.

Cuba plays an essential role in preserving the environment and promoting sustainability in the Caribbean. For example, it has *developed biodiversity protection programs and sustainable management of natural resources and promoted renewable energy sources.*

For the past twenty years, Cuba has remained one of the few remaining communist dictatorships in the world.

Castro's family ruled for over 60 years in Cuba: Fidel Castro ruled from 1959 to 2008, and his brother Raúl until 2018.

Raúl undertook some economic reforms during his tenure to stimulate private activity and attract foreign investment. Still, he also maintained control of political power and the mass media.

In INTERNATIONAL POLITICS, Cuba has continued to ally with countries such as Russia, China and Venezuela. However, the government has also sought to strengthen its relations with other countries, especially the United States. *In 2014, President Barack Obama began a process of normalising relations with Cuba, which involved reopening the U.S. embassy in Havana and the removal of some trade and travel restrictions.* However, with Donald Trump's arrival as president in 2017, these rapprochement efforts were partially reversed.

In terms of **INTERNATIONAL POLITICAL STRATEGY**, Cuba has sought to *promote international solidarity and socialist internationalism, primarily through its involvement in peace and international cooperation missions.* It also sought to encourage the unity of developing countries and resist the influence of the United States and Western countries.

To achieve these goals, Cuba has maintained close ties with countries such as Russia, China and Venezuela, which have shared a similar worldview and supported its government over the years. It has also sought to strengthen its relations with other developing countries and promote unity.

In addition, Cuba has participated in various peace and international cooperation missions through the United Nations and other international organizations. He has also supported global causes such as nuclear disarmament and the fight against climate change.

PART 4

WHAT ARE THE MILITARY EXPANSION POLICIES THAT MOST DESTABILIZE GLOBALLY?

In most of the general knowledge, you will surely hear several times about the concerns reported by the mainstream

media about the military expansion policies of Russia and the United States. *In short, let's look at them together.*

Russia's military expansion was mainly concentrated in the countries of the former Soviet bloc and neighbouring countries, such as Ukraine and Georgia.

Notably, Russia annexed Crimea from Ukraine in 2014 and supported pro-Russian separatists in eastern Ukraine, which led to an ongoing conflict that claimed thousands of lives.

Russia has also expressed its support for authoritarian regimes in other former Soviet bloc countries, such as Kazakhstan and Tajikistan.

Russia has expanded its military presence to other parts of the world, such as the Middle East and Africa. In the Middle East, Russia has supported Bashar al-Assad's regime in Syria and conducted military operations against rebel groups and jihadists.

In **Africa**, Russia has strengthened its relations with some countries, such as Egypt and the Democratic Republic of Congo, and opened a naval base in Eritrea.

The United States, on the other hand, has a global military presence and military bases in many countries worldwide, including **Germany, Japan, South Korea, Italy, and the United Kingdom**.

The United States has also conducted numerous military operations in different parts of the world. Such as **Afghanistan, Iraq and Syria,** often claiming to want to promote world peace and security and to defend the interests of the United States and its allies.

However, some critics argue that U.S. military expansion has helped create tensions and instability in different parts of the world. Therefore, the U.S. should be more cautious in promoting military intervention abroad.

Here is a concise list of areas where Russia and the United States have expanded their military presence in recent decades:

Russia:

1. *Eastern Europe:* Ukraine, Georgia, Kazakhstan, Tajikistan

2. *Middle East:* Syria

3. *Africa:* Egypt, Democratic Republic of Congo, Eritrea

United States:

1. *Europe*: Germany, Japan, Italy, United Kingdom

2. *Middle East:* Afghanistan, Iraq, Syria

3. *Asia:* Japan, South Korea

4. *Latin America*: Colombia, Honduras, Mexico

5. *Africa*: Somalia, Kenya, Ethiopia

6. Oceania: Australia, Guam, Philippines

But many other countries have increased their military presence in different parts of the world in recent decades. Still, the international community considers not all these developments worrying.

Some countries have significantly increased their military presence abroad in recent years. They have raised international concerns are China, India, Iran, North Korea and Turkey.

China has significantly increased its military presence abroad in recent years and has expanded its military presence in different parts of the world. Here is a summary of some of the areas where China has expanded its military presence:

1. **South China Sea: China** has built artificial islands in the South China Sea and equipped them with military infrastructure, such as airstrips and naval ports. China has also increased its naval presence in this region, raising concerns from the United States and other countries interested in the area.

2. **East China Sea: China** has increased its naval presence in the East China Sea and claimed sovereignty over several islands and atolls in the region. This raised concerns from Japan, South Korea and Taiwan.

3. China has developed military relations with many countries in **Asia, Africa and Latin America,** where it has increased its military presence in different parts of these regions.

Below is a concise list of the military expansion of India, North Korea and Turkey in recent years:

India:

1. Development of military relations with many countries in Asia, the Indian Ocean, Africa, Latin America and the Middle East.

2. The increased naval presence in the Indian Ocean.

3. Conducting military operations in different parts of Africa.

4. Development of naval and air bases in different parts of the world.

North Korea:

1. Development of a nuclear and missile program.

2. Increased military presence along the border with South Korea.

3. Conducting military exercises and missile tests.

Turkey:

1. Conducting military operations in Syria and Iraq.

2. Expansion of the naval presence in the Eastern Mediterranean.

3. Development of military relations with many countries in the Middle East.

Part 5

HOW USEFUL CAN GEOPOLITICS BE FOR ECONOMIC AND SOCIAL DEVELOPMENT?

Geopolitics can be very useful for a country's economic and social development in different ways. First, geopolitics can help to understand the political and economic dynamics at the global level, which can have an impact on the development of a country or region. Second, Geopolitics can provide crucial information on the availability of natural resources, trade flows and demographic changes, all of which can affect economic and social development.

Geopolitics can help identify opportunities for cooperation and development with other countries or regions through trade agreements, investment programs or cooperation projects. In addition, Geopolitics can help to understand the challenges and threats that a country or region may face, such as political instability or international tensions, and to develop strategies to address them.

Geopolitics can be very useful for a country's economic and social development. In addition, Geopolitics provides information and opportunities for developing trade relations and international cooperation and addressing challenges and threats.

Perhaps not everyone knows that

Geopolitics is not only applicable to Busi-

ness and Politics; in fact, there are many ar-

eas unknown to many in which it is used

Do we want to discover them together?

Then we start guessing.

CAN GEOPOLITICS HELP IN LITERATURE AND CINEMA?

Yes, geopolitics can help literature and cinema in several ways. For example, writers and filmmakers can use geopolitics to set their stories in a precise historical or geographical context and to make characters and events more believable and realistic. In addition, they can use geopolitics to explore themes such as international tensions, political instability or opportunities for cooperation and to develop plots and characters in a more in-depth and articulated way.

Geopolitics can help literature and film better understand the historical and cultural context in which stories are set and develop a greater awareness of global political and economic dynamics. In summary, geopolitics can be a valuable tool for writers and directors to put their stories in a realistic context and to develop more articulate and believable plots and characters.

Here are some examples of literary works that deal with geopolitics explicitly or implicitly:

1. "The Prince" by Niccolò Machiavelli: This political treatise explores how the principles of power and leadership can be applied to the geopolitical context of sixteenth-century Italy.

2. "The Man Without Qualities" by Robert Musil: This novel follows Ulrich, a man with no purpose in life, who lives in Vienna during the First World War. Geopolitics is a crucial element of history, as events are influenced by the geopolitical dynamics of the time.

3. "Human Beings" by Michel Houellebecq: This novel explores how globalization and economic integration have affected the geopolitics of Europe in the twenty-first century.

4. "Dune" by Frank Herbert: This science fiction novel follows Paul Atreides, a young man who becomes the leader of a powerful family that controls a desert planet. Geopolitics is an essential element of history, as events are influenced by the imaginary universe's geopolitical dynamics.

1. "The Hunger Games" by Suzanne Collins: This science fiction novel follows Katniss Everdeen, a young woman who participates in a deadly competition to represent her district in a dystopian society. Geopolitics is a crucial element of history, as events are influenced by the geopolitical dynamics of the imaginary society in which they occur.

For example, some television series that have dealt with geopolitics explicitly or implicitly and that have been positively received by audiences and critics include:

1.   "Homeland" by Howard Gordon and Alex Gansa

2.   "The Americans" by Joseph Weisberg

3.   "Madam Secretary" by Barbara Hall

4.   "Designated Survivor" by David Guggenheim

5.   "House of Cards" by Beau Willimon

6.   "The West Wing" by Aaron Sorkin

7.   "The Good Fight" by Robert King and Michelle King

8.   "The Man in the High Castle" by Frank Spotnitz

9.   "The Handmaid's Tale" by Bruce Miller

10.   "The Crown" by Peter Morgan

AND FOR SPORT?

Yes, sports can also be influenced by geopolitics in different ways.

For example, international relations can affect a country's or region's participation in international sporting events, such as the Olympic Games or the World Cup. In addition, political tensions or economic sanctions can impact the exchange of athletes or the organization of international sporting events.

Geopolitics can affect the spread and popularity of certain sports in different parts of the world, depending on a country or region's cultural traditions and economic development patterns.

In summary, geopolitics can be an essential factor to consider in the field of sports concerning the participation of a country or region in international sporting events and the spread and popularity of certain sports in different parts of the world.

GEOPOLITICS THEN...

Geopolitics deals with how political and economic dynamics, natural resources, populations, and cultures interact in a given geographical context and how these interactions can change over time.

Geopolitics deals with how relations between countries and regions of the world can change over time, depending on their resources, cultures, and political and economic strategies. In summary, geopolitics is a dynamic study that considers the past, present, and future relations between space, power, and conflict and how these relationships can change over time.

CONCLUSIONS

Geopolitics can be helpful to various actors at different levels and situations.

For example:

Governments: Governments can use geopolitics to better understand global political and economic dynamics and to

develop strategies to address the challenges and opportunities that come with them.

Businesses: Businesses can use geopolitics to identify investment opportunities, expand into new markets, and understand factors that could affect their business.

International organizations: International organizations, such as the UN or the EU, can use geopolitics to better understand global political and economic dynamics :

- to develop strategies
- to address the challenges and opportunities that arise from them.

Universities and research centres: Universities and research centres can use geopolitics to research and study factors that affect a country's economic and social development.

Individuals: Individuals can also benefit from geopolitics by better understanding global political and economic

dynamics and the opportunities and challenges that come with them and by developing strategies to address them.

Journalists can benefit from geopolitics in several ways.

For example, they can use geopolitics to better understand global political and economic dynamics and provide more accurate and comprehensive coverage. They can use geopolitics to identify the opportunities and challenges a country or region may face and provide insight into how these opportunities and challenges can affect people's daily lives. In addition, journalists can use geopolitics to understand the relationships and dynamics between different countries and regions of the world and to provide accurate and comprehensive coverage of international tensions and opportunities for cooperation. In summary, geopolitics can be helpful for journalists to give an accurate and extensive range of global political and economic dynamics and their implications for people.

"Geopolitics is like a global puzzle: each piece represents a country or region with a unique shape, colour and position.

Geopolitics helps us understand how these pieces interact with each other, depending on their resources, cultures and political and economic strategies.

And it also helps us predict how the puzzle might change in the future, depending on how the pieces move."

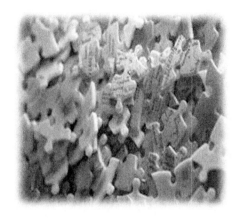

BIBLIOGRAPHY

"Geopolitics. The global dynamics of space and power" by Giampietro and Martellini

"Geopolitics for Beginners" by Mark Buchanan

"Understanding Geopolitics" by Gerard Chaliand and Jean-Pierre Rageau

"Geopolitics" by Klaus Dodds

"The Geopolitical": https://www.thegeopolitical.com/

"Geopolitical Futures": https://www.geopoliticalfutures.com/

"Foreign Affairs": https://www.foreignaffairs.com/

"Geopolitica.info": https://www.geopolitica.info/

"The Diplomat": https://thediplomat.com/

ABOUT THE AUTHOR

Antonella Silipigni writes books, which, considering where you're reading this, makes perfect sense.

She also writes non-fiction, on subjects ranging from personal finance to politics to poetry.

Antonella has long experiences in Politics, Marketing, Media Marketing, Sales, Teaching. She built up a reputation as a trusted freelancer, working for agencies and businesses alike.

After her stroke on 2018 due to a Cavernoma pontine she back to write as self publisher author.

In the pandemic she decided to back her love for poems and spiritual, social, political and economic topics. Witness of lot of stories and producer of mindful and wise ideas and words ready to share with you.

www.antonellasilipigni.com

Blog: www.CristinaChristine.com

Printed in Great Britain
by Amazon

43142062R00155